WHITE
SPIRITS

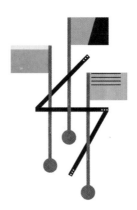

WHITE SPIRITS

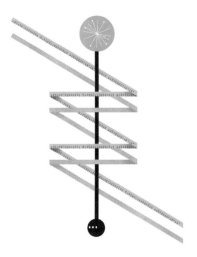

An innovative guide
to making 100 cocktails
using clear spirits: Gin, Vodka,
White Rum, Tequila, and more

DOG 'N' BONE

Published in 2015 by Dog 'n' Bone Books

An imprint of Ryland Peters & Small Ltd

20–21 Jockey's Fields   341 E 116th St
London WC1R 4BW   New York, NY 10029

www.rylandpeters.com

10 9 8 7 6 5 4 3 2 1

A CIP catalog record for this book is available from the
Library of Congress and the British Library.

ISBN: 978 1 909313 72 9

Printed in China

Designer: Paul Tilby
Editors: Helen Ridge and Pete Jorgensen
Photographer: Martin Norris
Illustrator: Blair Frame
Stylists: Michael Butt: pages 26–29, 38, 51–53, 69, 72,
77, 82–83, 87–88, 93–94, 100, 112, 125–127, 139
Andrew Shannon: pages 30–32, 35, 37, 39–49, 54–65,
70–71, 73–76, 78–81, 84–85, 90–92, 95–99, 101–105
Sevan Szekely: 34, 109–111, 113–124, 128–137, 140–143

Chapter 1: White Spirits Essentials text
by Michael Butt

RECIPE CREDITS

MICHAEL BUTT
Dry Martini p68
French 75 p72
Graham Greene p73
Gibson p74
Golden Gibson p75
Wibble p76
Southside p77
Bees Knees p78
Bramble p79
Albion p80
Space Gin Smash p81
Clover Club p82
Hedgerow Sling p83
White Lady p84
Ramos Fizz p85
Negroni p86
New Cross Negroni p88
Snow Angel p89
Soul Summer Cup p90
Forbidden Aperitif p91
Tom Collins p94
Velvet Sledgehammer p96
English Mojito p97
10CC p98
Raspari p100
Paloma p111
Grapefruit Cobbler p112
Daiquiri p82
Caribbean Flip p125
Mojito p126

BEN REED
French Martini p27
Bloody Mary p28
Raspberry Martini p31
Blood Martini p32
Legend p33
Joe Average p34
Madras p35
Metropolis p36
James Bond p37
Moscow Mule p38
Strawberry Mule p39
Black Russian p40
White Russian p41
Vodka Espresso p42
Claret Cobbler p45
Vodka Collins p47
Peach Rickey p48
Godchild p49
Cosmopolitan p52
Ginger Cosmo p54
Cosmo Royale p56
Cajun Martini p58
Polish Martini p59
Black Bison p60
Metropolitan p63
Tropical Breeze p64
Gimlet p70
Vesper p71
Red Snapper p93
Elderflower Collins p95
Raspberry Rickey p101
Margarita p108

Hemingway Daiquiri p123
Jamaican Breeze p134
Caipirinha p138
Azure Martini p141

WILLIAM YEOWARD
Apple Martini p58
Dragon p114
Brazilian Drum p143

LOUISE PICKFORD
Mandarin Caipiroska p44
Cosmo Iced Tea p55
Hollywood Hustle p62
Passionfruit Rum Punch p132

TONIA GEORGE
Sea Breeze p46

DOG 'N' BONE BOOKS
Vodka Martini p26
Raspberry Sour p57
Tatanka p61
Mandarin Mule p65
Gin and Tonic p92
Gin Sour p99
Aviation p102
Casino p103
Corpse Reviver No. 2 p105

Lagerita p110
Pepito Collins p113
El Diablo p115
Bloody Maria p116
Silk Stocking p117
Tequila Sunrise p118
Toreador p119
Strawberry Daiquiri p124
Pedro Collins p128
Cuba Libre p129
Mary Pickford p130
Piña Colada p131
Ti' Punch p133
Beachcomber p135
Raspberry Batida p140
Apricot Caipirinha p142

Contents

WHITE
SPIR
ESS

IT

NTIALS

Introduction

The process of fermentation is one of nature's great boons—the action of beneficent yeasts that allow bread to rise has provided the staff of life for millennia, but it is the evaporative by-product of this cornerstone-of-civilization reaction, ethanol, that interests us.

Since the very beginnings of distillation, the goal has been to make ever-purer spirit, and with guile and ingenuity we have finally succeeded. We can make spirit so pure that it is the perfect blank canvas for gin producers to showcase their botanicals and recipes without fear of distortion. We have learned to selectively capture the flavor and character of the raw materials, so that high-quality spirits around the world can be made with local ingredients and according to local distilling customs.

The number of choices that a distiller makes in his practice, coupled with the variety of possible ingredients, allows for an almost infinite range of wonderful products, from gin, vodka, tequila, and rum to cachaça or pisco. Welcome to the world of white spirits—whatever your poison, there will be a cocktail inside this book for you.

Making White Spirits

An explanation of the process of making the vast array of different spirits available can be quite daunting, just as standing in front of them, cash in hand at the liquor store can be. Over the last ten years, there has been a proliferation of new and interesting spirits, particularly gin, alongside an explosion in the popularity of cocktails. Understanding the "hows" and "whys" of the production process can be invaluable in helping you make a more informed choice when buying a bottle of your preferred white spirit. To crack the mystery of the art of spirit manufacture, it is easiest to start at the scene and work backward, just like a detective.

The Label

A huge amount of information about how a spirit is produced and its characteristics is given on the label. The proof or ABV (alcohol by volume) will be listed and, immediately, assumptions can be made about the spirit's character and style. All the categories of white spirit have rules defining their labeling—country of origin, distiller, as well as subcategory (London Dry or Old Tom Gin for example) of product can all be ascertained.

The Bottle

Fancy bottles cost money. Always bear in mind that when buying liquor, extravagant boxes and bottle presentations mean less of your money is inside the bottle.

Marrying

Manufacturers generally rest their distilled product after they have added water to it, as it helps to create a more rounded spirit—this process is sometimes referred to as marrying. The lower the ABV of the initial distillation product, the longer it will need to rest, but even vodka brands acknowledge that a relatively longer resting time is beneficial.

Dilution to Bottling Strength

The last process before bottling any white spirit is diluting it with water to bring the distilled product down to a standard bottling strength. This is an important step and, generally, 50–60% of the bottle is water. Most spirit producers use deionized water for this, to ensure consistency and safety, as municipal water sources are of insufficient quality. Deionized water tastes strange because the body is not conditioned to enjoy things that are less saline than itself.

Dissolved mineral salts give mineral waters their different characters, and there are some vodka and gin producers who believe that unfiltered water brings a more natural finish to their final spirit. Examples of these worth trying include Reyka, 42 Below, and Finlandia vodkas, which are all excellent.

Aging

The barrel-aging of a spirit is something associated with brown spirits, but a significant number of white rums are also aged in barrels and then filtered back so they are colorless. This takes advantage of the mellowing effect of maturation without adding significant flavor.

Flavoring

White spirits are often flavored after distillation. The two biggest categories of cocktails in this book—gin and vodka—are both based on flavored spirits. Producers can proceed down three routes when flavoring spirits.

• The traditional flavored vodkas, including the Polish trio of Zubrowka, Cytrynowka, and Krupnik, are all made by infusing the neutral spirit with combinations of herbs, spices, honey, and fruit. Once the infusion process is complete, the material is strained out. Often these spirits take on some color from the infused ingredients, so are technically no longer white—but they are very tasty.

• The second method is to flavor the spirit with essences, which are concentrated tinctures made by extracting individual chemical compounds from natural materials. These building blocks of flavor are then assembled in a process resembling the work of a parfumier, in an attempt to accurately match the original fruit or herb. This process is commonly used on most flavored vodka, as well as cheap gin. The organic chemist can get close to perfection in their blends, so although this technique is less "artisanal," the variation in quality of comparable products demonstrates there is significant skill used in the process.

• Distilled gin, London Dry Gin, Plymouth Gin—all these appellations define legally that the product inside the bottle is flavored by a distillation process. Gin (and some more expensive flavored vodkas) is made by steeping the botanical ingredients in quantities specified in a recipe for a prescribed length of time, and then redistilling them to capture the infused botanicals. Gin can also be produced with vapor-based infusion using a specific still, a process that extracts a lighter set of flavors.

Filtration

The discovery of activated charcoal filtration revolutionized the production of white spirits. Activated carbon has the ability to bind with a huge array of organic chemicals and, due to its surface area (1g has a surface area equivalent to that of two tennis courts), is an amazingly effective filter of undesirable components of a distilled product. With current state-of-the-art distillation apparatus, charcoal filtration is not always required, but its historical impact in the creation of modern vodka and gin categories has been large. Charcoal filtration is, however, very much a part of the creation of other white spirits today, particularly rum.

Chill filtering is used primarily in the production of aged spirits to prevent clouding when they are bottled at less than 43% ABV. The marketing departments of vodka companies have jumped on the filtration process in the production of the spirit, with claims of using diamond dust, gold, quartz, and various other esoteric materials. Suffice to say that the vast majority of these claims are "enthusiastic" at best, with the filtering effect limited to a simple mechanical one that would remove only the very largest of molecules.

Distillation

Distillation can be defined as the concentration of a liquid by selective evaporation and condensation. The process of a liquid evaporating and condensing would have been observed the first time someone put the lid on a pan of soup, and there is evidence that the jump to collecting only a part of the condensate happened at least 4,000 years ago.

POT STILLS

Fermented alcohol was readily available the world over but it was not until the Moors landed in southern Europe with an effective pot still in the 8th century CE that the process of creating potable distilled alcohol began. The concentration of alcohol in the solution through distillation relies on the fact that water and ethanol boil at different temperatures: ethanol at 173.1°F (78.37°C) and water at 212°F (100°C). This means that in a mixture of the two, the ethanol will boil first and be collected before the water begins to boil.

At its most basic, a pot still is really just a kettle, with a spout to collect the vapors, and a cooled "worm" pipe to condense the steam.

The fermented mix of alcohol, water, yeast, and the residual compounds of the raw material is placed in the kettle. Heat is applied and, as the temperature approaches 173.1°F (78.37°C), the condensate is collected. The condensate formed at lower temperatures will contain more volatile compounds and methanol; these are known as the "heads" and are discarded. (Methanol, which can be

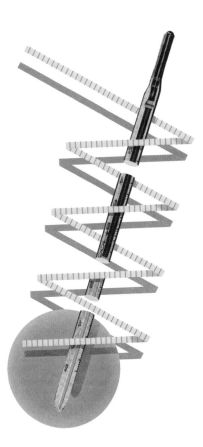

beginning of the process. If that was all there was to it, there would be no problem in using a pot still to produce very high concentrations of ethanol. The problem comes with our understanding of temperature. Temperature is an expression of molecular kinetic energy, or how quickly molecules are vibrating in a solid or moving in a liquid or gas.

When we measure temperature, we are measuring the mean kinetic energy for all the molecules in the system, but a molecule changes state when its individual kinetic energy exceeds the melting or boiling point of the substance. In a solution, individual molecules of the same substance will have different kinetic energy, the spread of which conforms to a normal distribution—a bell-shaped symmetrical curve where most readings occur around the mean (the total of the readings divided by the number) and tail off away from the mean.

This means that, at any given temperature, some more volatile compounds with a theoretically lower boiling point will have a kinetic energy lower than the mean will be in the sample, alongside heavier and less volatile molecules that happened to have a higher than average kinetic energy. The overlaps of the normal distribution of all the different compounds in the mash mean that even at exactly 173.1°F (78.37°C), the distiller will not collect only ethanol from the still. While it is theoretically possible to redistill eight or nine times using a pot still, thereby producing a very pure spirit, this is never done in practice. The maximum distillation efficiency for a pot still in commercial use is around 75% ABV.

produced in some quantity by fermentation, boils at a significantly lower temperature than ethanol, at 148.5°F (64.7°C), and its accidental inclusion by home distillers in the collected portion of the distillate is the cause of blindness and a large number of deaths every year—as small a dose as 1¾oz (50ml) is lethal. As a home distiller once put it, "First the white stick and the dog, then you die.")

The condensate is collected from temperatures around that of ethanol's boiling point. As the temperature increases further, the condensate changes to less volatile alcohols and other organic compounds, then, of course, water. These are known as the "tails" and are normally returned to the

CONTINUOUS DISTILLATION

Continuous distillation was perfected in the 1820s and it allowed, for the first time, alcohol to be produced at a much higher ABV. Created primarily as a device to speed up the production of alcohol and lower the cost, continuous stills, as suggested by their name, can run continuously, whereas pot distillation is a batch process, with the still requiring lengthy cleaning between distillations.

At its simplest, the continuous still is a pair of columns: the analyzer and the rectifier.

The process is most easily demonstrated with a diagram of a simplified arrangement (see below)—continuous stills used to create neutral grain spirit are often far more complex than this, with multiple rectifying columns resembling a rocket factory more than the traditional image of a distillery.

The bit that interests us is the ability that the plates in each rectifier have to selectively condense much more accurate fractions of the distillate than

ANALYSER   RECTIFIER

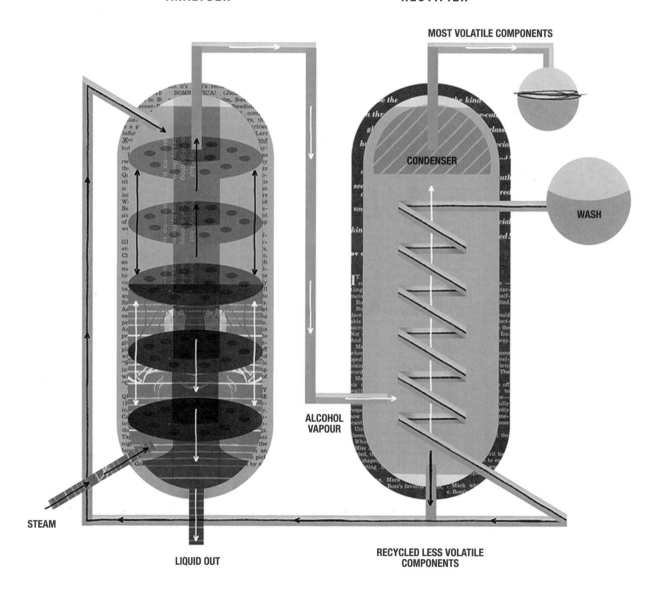

MOST VOLATILE COMPONENTS

CONDENSER

WASH

ALCOHOL VAPOUR

STEAM

LIQUID OUT

RECYCLED LESS VOLATILE COMPONENTS

can be achieved in a pot still. Each plate effectively acts a micro-distillation, removing further components. Simple continuous stills have the ability to distill to 95.6% ABV, limited by the azeotropic (a liquid mixture containing two or more substances which boils without decomposition, thus preventing separation) behavior of ethanol and water, whose boiling points merge at high ethanol concentrations in the mixture. More complex stills can use variations in pressure to raise ABV, but for practical purposes a spirit is classed as neutral grain spirit at 95% ABV.

So, what makes up the rest of the distillate? Mainly water, and a very limited number of congeners, or flavor molecules, in tiny concentrations. The entire vodka industry relies on the implication that you can detect and savor these congeners, and that they are characteristic of a producer's raw material and distillation technique. In conducted tests, however, it is very difficult to ascribe any ability for even trained experts to identify or characterize different brands with any statistical significance.

Fermentation

Yeast is vital for converting the soluble sugars into alcohol and carbon dioxide during the fermentation process, which is great for bakers, brewers, and distillers, but not necessarily for the yeast. Alcohol is an unwanted by-product of the yeast's respiration and will eventually kill the yeast when it reaches high-enough concentrations. During its life cycle and the fermentation

process, yeast generates other alcohols and organic chemicals, and as the yeast itself is included in the mash that goes into a continuous or pot still, all of the compounds that make up the organism can play a part in the final taste of the spirit. The strain of yeast and the length of fermentation are said by distillers to be the "thumbprint" of the spirit, which is virtually impossible to replicate using different yeasts or processes.

Raw Materials

White spirits can be made from just about anything, and a good liquor store will have spirits made from agave, apples, barley, cherries, grapes, maize, molasses, pears, plums, potatoes, rye, raspberries, rice, sugar beet, sugar cane, wheat, and possibly a couple more. The contribution of the raw materials in making the final spirit depends very much on the final ABV of the distillation. Less ethanol means more flavor compounds from the raw materials.

When vodka or neutral grain spirit is taken up to 95% ABV pure, it is difficult to ascertain the source of any of the flavors in such low concentrations. It is much easier to see the effect in brandies like pisco or eau de vie, which come off the still at 70% ABV expressing a lot of character of the base ingredients. Cachaça and tequila, which come off the still at 55% ABV, exhibit the clearest references to the raw material.

Raw materials that have soluble sugars suitable for distillation will bring

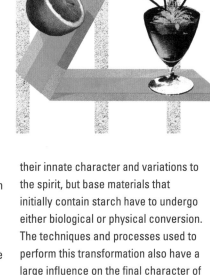

their innate character and variations to the spirit, but base materials that initially contain starch have to undergo either biological or physical conversion. The techniques and processes used to perform this transformation also have a large influence on the final character of the spirit.

Combining all these opportunities for variation gives us the huge range of white spirits available today, and each chapter of the book will look into the elements that particularly influence the specific category. Alongside some drinking "research," this will give you a much better understanding of both how a product is made and what you can do with it. Enjoy learning!

All in the Nose—how to taste and assess liquor

The most difficult skill in technical bartending is certainly training the senses of smell and taste to become tools; we have an amazing olfactory system, capable of distinguishing ingredients as diffuse as 5ppm (parts per million). But where do you start? Everyone has the ability to connect sensations with remembered things, times, and places. That is why when you first smell a spirit or wine you may find the things in your head are not necessarily just about food. The first thing you need to do is interrogate your palate, trying to discern the different elements that make up the taste profile. These will, in the beginning, have little outside reference; they are your thoughts after all. The next step is to start to build taste profiles more in terms of the whole product. This is needed to truly grade and identify compared spirits. This is all really hard and can take a lifetime to answer. The longest journey starts with a first step. When tasting beers, wine, and spirits it is good to take a systematic approach to recording the results. It not only makes rating and comparing spirits easier on a direct basis, but also allows you to compare products tasted at different times.

TASTING

The first taste is with the eye—look at the bottle if you can. This will give you a reference to its ABV and how that influences the spirit. It will also give you a ballpark of tastes to work with.

Now to the product—again use your eyes. Firstly, is it free of foreign bodies? These generally mean that the product might be corrupted and tasting worthless. Now on to the color. There is a huge range of specified colors used in tasting but you can make up your own.

The color can tell you a lot about certain products, giving clues about aging, depth of flavor, or additives. It is most useful when attempting to compare similar products.

SWIRL the wine or spirit—look how the liquid returns to the level, leaving characteristic trails or legs (tears). These can give a good idea of the relative viscosities of liquids. In spirits long legs mean high sugar, high alcohol.

SWIRL AGAIN to release the aroma—this requires a tasting or wine glass to ensure the aroma is contained. Here is the first major mistake—DO NOT stick your nose in and sniff! The alcohol will completely desensitize your nose for about ten minutes. Gently approach the glass until the first aromas are apparent; retreat and then slowly proceed to get closer. It is often said that if you breathe through your mouth close to the glass, the aroma will travel up the back of the nose (this does work!)

ASSESS THE AROMA—light and fruity, zesty, or more complex? Are there any obvious flavors that you can identify, is there a dominating flavor, or is it more balanced?

NOW FOR THE TASTE—be careful here, there is no need to take in much liquid, we don't want to desensitize the mouth either. Generally, the best way is to place a small amount on the tongue and let it heat up and evaporate as it moves around the mouth. Remember you have taste buds all around your tongue, so make sure the spirit passes around the mouth.

ASSESS THE TASTE—to do this it is easiest to split it into sections; initial, mid palate and mouth feel. These can show how the spirit develops after you get the primary taste. Remember, smell is just able to access the airborne component of the drink and these most volatile flavors are often the lighter notes, while the deeper undertones will arrive when the spirit has warmed up in the mouth.

BALANCE IS KEY—as with everything in life. The spirit should have a round and full profile with discernible character. The mouth feel is also important. Does the spirit fill the mouth or taste a bit thin and watery? Even when tasting vodkas, mouth feel is probably the biggest clue as to what is going on.

THE FINISH—this is not just the burn when the spirit passes down your throat. You don't even have to swallow. Finish is more about the lasting impression you are getting from your senses. Is the finish pleasant or harsh? How long is it? Some Cognacs will have finishes lasting tens of minutes.

THE REASSESS—if you are tasting comparatively then you should always go back to anything you are unsure about, as you will set boundaries and comparisons with the other examples—one brandy might have hints of apple, as might another, while another still might have more prominent pear flavors. Without checking back, accurate comparisons can't be achieved.

The process is always a learning one. The best way is to design a system to record your tasting notes in a permanent manner, in a style that is consistent across all the tastings you do. You will find that you will quickly build quite a reference guide and also a vocabulary of taste to work with.

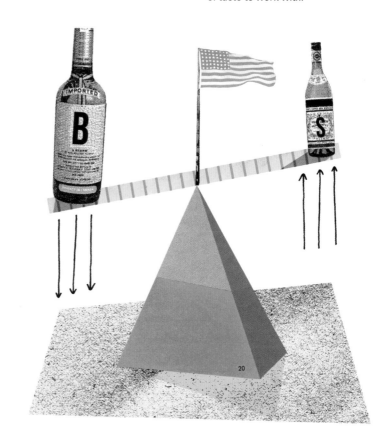

Essential Equipment

You can make cocktails almost anywhere, and there is no need to spend a lot of money on fancy equipment. If you look around your kitchen I bet you will find at least ten specialist items you never use, from fondue sets to bread makers, mandolins and the clever little gadget for cutting the top off a boiled egg. Cocktails can be shaken in Kilner jars and vacuum flasks, strained with a pasta fork, and stirred with a pencil (pencils actually make the coldest martinis), but if you are even remotely serious about making drinks at home it is worth assembling a set of basic bar tools. They will make your life easier and your drinks better.

Glassware

The majority of the drinks in this book can be served in one of four glasses:

COCKTAIL GLASS—sometimes wrongly called a martini glass after its most famous occupant. The standard size is around 7oz (200ml).

LARGE, SHORT WHISKEY TUMBLER— often called a double old-fashioned glass, of around 12oz (330ml).

HIGHBALL GLASS—around 14oz (400ml)

WINE GLASS

If you are making drinks only for yourself, then it is perfectly acceptable to just buy one of each, but hopefully with your new found mixology skills your company will be much in demand and therefore it is sensible to buy a set of matching glasses in each category. Buy glasses that you like and look after them. Wine aficionados will tell you that glass shape and rim thickness have a large impact on how a wine "presents" and it is true, so try and get good ones. Note that cocktail glasses in particular vary massively in size so larger ones may require some adaptation of the recipes—and a tougher liver.

Garnish Tools

"The first sip is with the eye" is all too true—a well made drink can be made amazing with just a little care and some artistic finishing touches. Most garnishes are made with a knife (see page 21) but there are a couple of cheap tools that can make it easier to deliver perfect looking cocktails.

CANELLE KNIFE—often known as a zesting knife, this tool cuts a thin ribbon of zest from a citrus fruit that can then be knotted or made into a spiral. If you want to make slightly larger citrus twists to finish your drinks a good-quality potato peeler works very well.

FINE GRATER—used to grate chocolate, cinnamon, or nutmeg at the last minute to release the aroma of spices. It is worth buying a good-quality laser-cut grater as the old-style punched-steel box graters are much less effective.

COCKTAIL STICKS—you can, of course, just use wooden ones, but for a little je ne sais quoi consider getting a set of decorative cocktail sticks. Available in glass, steel, or even silver, they are not expensive and really make a difference.

Just make sure they are long enough to work with your chosen glassware.

Strainers

There are three types of strainer used to make cocktails, the most important of which is the hawthorne or variable strainer. As with all strainers the purpose is to separate the drink from the ice and any solid components of the drink.

HAWTHORNE STRAINER—consisting of a perforated plate with handle and a spring, most designs allow the two pieces to be separated for easy cleaning. To use a hawthorne strainer, place it in the top of the tin of the Boston shaker (see page 20), spring inward. Your finger should fall naturally on the small tab in the centre. When straining drinks over ice, the drink can then be simply poured into the glass. When straining drinks that are served straight up, push the tab on the strainer downwards, this compresses the spring, making the apertures between the coils smaller and removing any small shards of ice that have been created while shaking.

H

JULEP STRAINER—originally designed to keep fragments of mint inside the glass when drinking a mint Julep, this tool is fantastic for pouring stirred drinks from the Boston glass. It allows for a smoother pour, with no spillage. Simply place the strainer inside the glass at a 45-degree angle, hold the handle steady by wrapping the index finger around it, and pour.

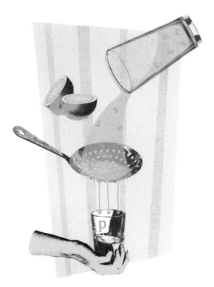

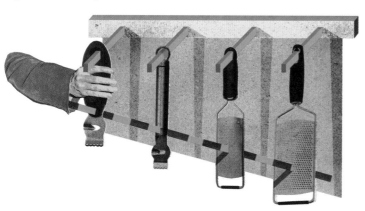

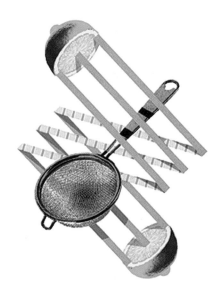

STANDARD SHAKER—the original shaker basically has three parts—a tin, a straining cap, and a lid. These shaker sets are used more rarely now as the compression seals between sections have to be highly engineered and therefore expensive before they work properly.

BOSTON SHAKER—these became more popular in the late 40s. The Boston shaker consists of a tempered glass mixing vessel and a stainless steel tin. This is the tool most professional bartenders choose to use as it gives the most flexibility and is quick to use. It is a little harder to master than a standard shaker but certainly worth the practice.

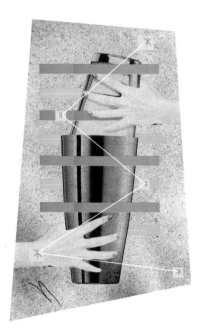

To use a Boston shaker first place all the ingredients in the glass half, this gives you a useful secondary check on your measuring. Next fill the glass with ice; the amount used will affect the

FINE STRAINER—similar to a tea strainer but with a larger gauge mesh (1⁄16in/1mm), this strainer is often used with a hawthorne strainer to completely remove any shards of ice or small fragments of fruit and herbs that might spoil the appearance of the drink. To use, place the hawthorne in the Boston tin as normal and pour the liquid through the fine strainer into the glass.

Shakers

The most important piece of equipment for producing cocktails is obviously the cocktail shaker. There are two main categories of shaker, although as they have always been seen as decorative items there are thousands of different designs, from the simple to the outright bizarre. Antiques fairs, flea markets, and of course the Internet are great places to find interesting and beautiful variations.

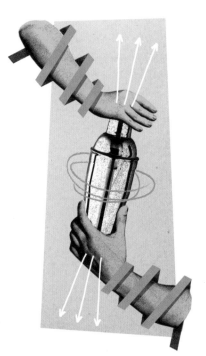

dilution of the drink so it is important to be consistent. The easiest way to do this is always to fill it to the very top. Next place the Boston tin on top of the glass and press down gently. The ice inside will very quickly chill the air, causing it to contract and form a seal between the two halves. You can check the seal by picking the shaker up by the tin. The glass should be stuck to it.

Shaking requires effort! Holding each half of the shaker in each hand, shake as hard as you can for 10 seconds, the idea being that the ice and liquid travel from one end of the shaker to the other, crashing against the ends, mixing the liquid while chilling and diluting it.

To open the shaker, reverse the position so the tin is on the bottom, grasp both halves in your non-dominant hand and gently tap the protruding brim of the metal half with the heel of your hand to break the seal, if it doesn't break easily, try rotating 90 degrees.

Preparation Tools

Most of the work in making cocktails comes before the shaking—prepping your ingredients and measuring. Many of the tools required are already in your kitchen, but there are a few extras you will need.

BARSPOON—used for two purposes: stirring drinks and layering. Layering has two approaches: for non-mixable spirits such as Kahlua and Baileys the flat end can be rested on the surface of the liquid and the ingredient poured gently down the stem of the spoon. For more troublesome combinations like Baileys and Grand Marnier, it is better to rest the bowl of the spoon cup-side up and pour the liquid into this to slow the flow right down.

SPIRIT MEASURES—throughout the book the recipes are defined in parts, to save any confusion with different measuring systems. A part can be anything from a spirit measure, a shot glass, or an egg cup. It is worth buying a set of professional spirit measures, either in multiples of ounces or 25 milliliters. They make measuring half parts much easier and allow you to use corresponding measuring spoons for small quantities. It is also useful to have a graduated measuring jug/cup for larger quantities, especially if you are making drinks for friends.

MUDDLER—this is simply a stick for crushing fruits and releasing the essential oils and aromas from herbs. You can easily substitute a rolling pin without handles for this purpose, but if you are planning to make a lot of fresh fruit drinks, a proper muddling stick with engineered points or ridges will make the process easier and faster.

JUICER—you will need a juicer for any drinks using citrus juices. Any style is fine; some food processors come with an attachment or you can buy an electric one for not too much money. I still like to use a hand juicer for most cocktails but if you are making drinks for a party it is easier to use an electric one. NEVER buy pre-juiced lemon or lime juice—they all taste disgusting.

KNIVES—these are often overlooked but they are the most important piece of equipment, and the one that takes the most time to master. Most bar knives fall into two categories: serrated and plain-bladed. Serrated blades are very useful for cutting citrus fruits as the sawing motion used will easily cut through tough skins. Also, for preparing citrus twists a serrated blade is much better for pith removal. Straight-edged blades are more useful to a bartender in dealing with softer fruits and where a particularly fine edge is required.

When using any knife make sure you have a cutting board to protect you and your surfaces. This allows a firm base to any cut stroke. If you are having difficulty cutting round fruits, cut a section from the end to form a flat and stable base; a good bar knife should be a 4–6in (10–15cm) long, flexible paring knife. The only time you may need a bigger knife is to cut watermelons or large pineapples. When cutting large objects, use a knife big enough that you can see the tip and the heel all the way through the cutting stroke.

Any knife you use must be very sharp so keep a sharpener at hand. Sharp knives not only make nicer looking garnishes with precise edges, they are easier and quicker to use. In the event of an accident, injuries from sharp knives are usually less severe because less driving pressure is required for the cutting stroke. Most however, occur because of carelessness or misuse. You only get one set of hands so take care of them. Take your time and practice until you feel comfortable.

EXTRAS—once you, and more importantly your friends, have realized that you like making cocktails there are a number of other tools that are worth purchasing. Consider investing in an egg white separator, a pineapple corer, an olive/cherry pitter, crushed ice maker, and large insulated ice bucket to complete your home bar set up.

Home Bar Ingredients

The first mistake people make when setting up a home bar, or even just planning a cocktail party, is going to a liquor store or off-licence and buying lots of booze, which then just sits unused in the drinks cabinet, gathering dust and oxidizing. The best bottles to buy are obviously different types of white spirit and strong booze does not noticeably deteriorate if kept properly.

There are, however, some staples that are worth buying and keeping in stock; you never know when you or your guests might fancy a cocktail.

In the liquor cabinet

ORANGE LIQUEUR

A vital ingredient in lots of cocktails, a good-quality orange liqueur will allow you to make great rum drinks, margaritas, and much more. I would recommend always having a bottle of Cointreau in stock, as it will also work in all the recipes that require triple sec or orange Curaçao. If you love rum drinks though it is definitely worth getting an orange Curaçao. Pierre Ferrand makes the very best but any brand that bottles at 35–40 percent will be of good quality. Some drinks work well with aged orange liqueurs like Grand Marnier, so if you fancy picking up a bottle it will serve you well. As a bonus, good orange liqueurs can be enjoyed on their own with a bit of ice.

ANGOSTURA BITTERS

There has been an explosion in the number of aromatic bitters available on the market in recent years, with lots of companies across the globe producing a variety of different styles, based on almost every type of ingredient you can think of. Although not the oldest, to my mind the best is Angostura, made in Trinidad and Tobago. With its immediately recognizable packaging it is an absolute requirement in every commercial bar and should also be in every home bar. By all means experiment with other styles of bitters—visits to a good cocktail bar will enable you to try some of the more esoteric ones. Buy a bottle if you like them—they don't deteriorate and are normally sold in small sizes.

SWEET AND DRY VERMOUTH

Vermouth is fortified, aromatized wine, sweetened with sugar or grape must. There are many varieties on the market, each with its own proprietary blend of herbs and ingredients. Most commonly associated with France and Italy, the producing companies often sell a range of styles of vermouth, from dry white through to bold red wine-based versions. If you like Martinis, buying a dry style can make sense, but as it is used in small quantities in drinks and oxidizes just like wine, the bottle in the cupboard or home bar often goes off. Sweet vermouth is used in far more cocktails and in larger quantities so there is less danger of spoilage, but once open it is worth keeping them in the fridge. Martini and Rossi is probably the most famous manufacturer but I prefer the French producer Lillet, which although a little more expensive is very versatile and lovely to drink on its own. Some bartenders swear by Punt e Mes or their Antica Formula variety; some love the quinine in Dubonnet, but if you really fancy a treat, try and search out a bottle of Barolo Chinato by Cocchi. I promise you will not be disappointed.

CAMPARI AND APEROL

The most famous of the bitters, Campari is an acquired taste, as the bitter notes are very strong. It is definitely worth persevering though as it is a truly wonderful aperitif on its own and also a vital ingredient in the Negroni. If you fancy easing in gently, Aperol is a slightly less bitter equivalent with a more pronounced orange note.

CHAMBORD

A black raspberry liqueur made in France, this make works well with lots of spirits. When mixed with Champagne it makes a great Kir Imperiale.

CRÈME DE CASSIS AND CRÈME DE MURE

These two liqueurs, made from blackcurrants and blackberries respectively, have a great depth of flavor and are key ingredients in cocktails such as the Graham Greene and the Bramble. Like Chambord, a dash of these liqueurs is also a great addition to a glass of Champagne.

COFFEE LIQUEUR

A great addition to the liquor cabinet, useful for making simple coffee cocktails and great on its own as a digestif. Kahlua and Tia Maria are easily available and delicious, but Toussaint and Galliano Ristretto are excellent boutique variations.

In the pantry

EGGS

Whilst not strictly an ingredient for the pantry, it's always handy to stock a few fresh eggs in the refrigerator. Adding egg white to your cocktails will add texture thanks to the proteins found in the whites stretching to produce a thick, creamy foam that looks stunning. Be sure to dry shake egg whites first without ice, it produces a more impressive head. It's a simple trick but one that your guests will love.

CHERRIES

Cocktail cherries and Maraschino cherries are generally pretty unpleasant—anything with that unnatural a color generally tastes too artificial. Instead look for black or morello cherries in syrup. Alternatively, preserve your own cherries while they are in season—if you use your favorite brown booze as part of the preserving liquor they will taste even better.

ELDERFLOWER CORDIAL

Great when mixed with water, but even better in cocktails! Given its floral nature, it works particularly well with the botanical in gin. A relatively new addition to the cocktail world is an elderflower liqueur called St Germain, which has become an increasingly common ingredient on menus at some of the world's top bars.

Prepared ingredients

SIMPLE SYRUP

You can buy sugar syrup from a good off-licence or liquor store but making your own at home is easy and much cheaper. Simply mix water and superfine (caster) sugar in equal quantities by weight and stir. It will be cloudy at first but keep stirring and eventually it will form a clear syrup. This will keep in the fridge for 3 weeks.

JUICE

Easily the most important ingredient (apart from the booze) in the vast majority of cocktails is the lemon and lime juice. Never buy pasteurized juice—it tastes horrible. An electric juicer is a great investment, especially if you are making batches of cocktails for a party, but you can cater for about ten people with only a hand juicer. Once squeezed, lemon and lime juice will last for just 48 hours, so if in doubt, squeeze fresh for every cocktail.

VOD

Vodka Martini

While the original Martini was made over a century ago using gin as the key ingredient, in recent times vodka has become a popular alternative. It makes sense, after all gin is effectively vodka infused with various botanicals. Given that gin came first, there is a detailed profile on how to make a Martini on page 63. This version is a little punchier than the gin alternative, choosing a balance of 8 parts vodka to 1 part dry vermouth, but experiment with the ratios to find your perfect version. And be sure to serve it ice cold.

8 parts vodka
1 part dry vermouth
Garnish: Pitted olives
on a cocktail stick/
toothpick or lemon zest

Fill a mixing glass with ice and stir with a barspoon until the glass is chilled. Tip the water out and top with ice. Add a dash of dry vermouth and the vodka and stir in a continuous circular motion until the liquid is thoroughly chilled. Strain into a frosted cocktail glass and garnish with either pitted olives or a lemon zest.

French Martini

While cocktail purists may question the legitimacy of this drink's claim to be included under the Martini banner, the French Martini is great for parties as it is light, fruity, and simple to make in bulk.

2 parts vodka
½ part raspberry liqueur
3 parts fresh pineapple juice
Garnish: 3 raspberries on a cocktail stick/toothpick or a pineapple wedge

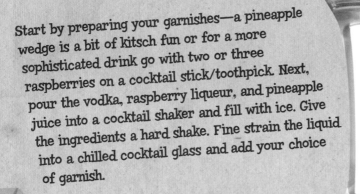

Start by preparing your garnishes—a pineapple wedge is a bit of kitsch fun or for a more sophisticated drink go with two or three raspberries on a cocktail stick/toothpick. Next, pour the vodka, raspberry liqueur, and pineapple juice into a cocktail shaker and fill with ice. Give the ingredients a hard shake. Fine strain the liquid into a chilled cocktail glass and add your choice of garnish.

Bloody Mary

1 part vodka

4 parts tomato juice

2 pinches of freshly ground black pepper

2 dashes of Worcestershire sauce

2 dashes of Tabasco

2 dashes of lemon juice

1 barspoon horseradish sauce

Garnish: Celery stick and a lemon wedge

GLASSWARE:

When it comes to hair of the dog cocktails, the Bloody Mary is the queen that reigns over them all. Over the years this savory cocktail has probably caused as many hangovers as it has allegedly cured, but there is something inherently comforting about sipping on one the morning after a big night out. Like that other classic, the Martini, this is a drink that rewards a bit of tinkering, so play around with the spicing and savoury elements to work out what your ultimate version is.

Ask for a Bloody Mary in a pub and often it will be assembled in front of you in the glass with very little in the way of extras apart from a pepper pot waved vaguely in the direction of the drink and a dash of Tabasco. This isn't the way to do it! Instead, add all the ingredients to a shaker filled with ice. Shake gently and strain into a highball glass topped with ice. Garnish with a celery stick and lemon wedge. If you're making the drink for other people, offer them the option of adding some extra flavor, but in many eyes this recipe is hard to beat.

1 part apple schnapps
2 parts vodka
1 parts apple juice
½ part fresh lime juice
½ part simple syrup
Garnish: Thinly sliced
apple fan

GLASSWARE:

Apple Martini

It's not hard to see why this drink is always a crowd pleaser—
the crispness of the apple acts as an excellent foil to the vodka,
while the sharpness of the lime makes your
tastebuds stand to attention only to be soothed
into submission by the sweet-talking sugar syrup.

Put the ingredients in a cocktail shaker filled with ice.
Shake the contents for around 15 seconds until you
feel condensation around the shaker and strain
into a cocktail glass. Garnish with an apple fan.

When creating your apple fan garnish, make sure you
cut the slices just before you start making the drink.
Freshly cut slices will "stick" together ready to be
placed on the edge of the glass.

Raspberry Martini

2 parts vodka
Dash of raspberry liqueur
Dash of orange bitters
½ part raspberry purée
(or a handful of raspberries)
Garnish: Raspberry and
a lemon slice

Another fruity variation on the Martini theme, this time with raspberries. This version should be quite thick in consistency, so if you aren't using pre-made purée, use a good handful of raspberries to ensure it flows down your neck like treacle.

Add all the ingredients to a cocktail shaker filled with ice. If using fresh raspberries, place them in the shaker first and muddle to release the juices, then add the remaining ingredients. Shake sharply and fine strain into a frosted cocktail glass to remove any seeds from the fruit and give you a smoother drink. Garnish with a fresh raspberry and a slice of lemon on a cocktail stick/toothpick.

Blood Martini

3 parts vodka
1 part Campari
½ part raspberry liqueur
¼ part fresh lime juice
2 parts cranberry juice
Dash of Cointreau
Garnish: orange peel or
flaming orange zest

A bittersweet concoction that needs to be delicately balanced as there are quite a few ingredients involved. The lime and the Campari provide the bitterness, while the sweet element comes in the form of the raspberry liqueur. Campari is an ingredient that can take a bit of getting used to—there are not many people who try their first Negroni and claim to adore it. This drink is a good way to introduce your palate to its bitterness.

Add all the ingredients to a cocktail shaker filled with ice. Shake sharply and strain into a frosted cocktail glass. Garnish with an orange zest, twisting to release the oils, or, if you've got the skills, flame the orange zest (see page 52). Taste the drink before and after adding the orange zest—what a difference!

Legend

2 parts vodka
1 part blackberry liqueur
1 part fresh lime juice
Dash of simple syrup
(see page 23)

GLASSWARE:

Invented in London in the late 1980s, this recipe has to be followed closely as too much of any of the ingredients can result in an unpalatable cocktail. Balance is the key, so make sure you taste each concoction before you serve it.

Add all the ingredients to a cocktail shaker and fill it with ice. Give the ingredients a good, sharp shake to cool the liquid before straining into a chilled cocktail glass.

6 parts vodka
½ part Pimm's No. 1
Garnish: Lemon zest and
a cucumber wheel

Joe Average

GLASSWARE:

Pimm's is most commonly associated with civilized English summer garden parties and croquet on the lawn, but don't let its inclusion in the recipe fool you—this is not a drink to be taken lightly. By pairing the Pimm's with a sizeable measure of vodka, the ingredient is given the chance to demonstrate its unruly side. The addition of the lemon and cucumber garnishes is a little tip of the straw boater to Pimm's more usual accompaniments.

Add both the ingredients to a mixing glass filled with ice. Stir the contents carefully to dilute the ice slightly and decrease the potency of the vodka. Once the outside of the glass appears frosted the drink is ready to serve. Strain the liquid into a pre-chilled cocktail glass and garnish with a thin wheel of cucumber and a lemon zest.

Madras

Why this cocktail is named Madras is a mystery, but it's especially refreshing when created with fresh orange juice. This is a real easy drinker and one to be savored when temperatures reach the levels you'd find on the Indian sub-continent. Or perhaps it will become the mouth cooler of choice for anyone who has ingested a particularly fiery curry!

2 parts vodka
3 parts cranberry juice
3 parts fresh orange juice
Garnish: orange slice

Pour the vodka into a highball glass filled with ice. Top with equal amounts of cranberry juice and orange juice and garnish with a slice of orange. Serve with a straw.

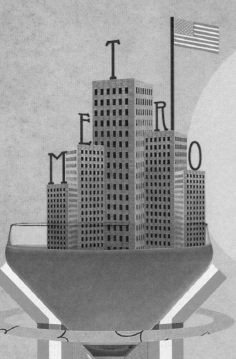

1 part vodka
1 part raspberry liqueur
Champagne, to top up

Metropolis

GLASSWARE:

The Metropolis was a logical creation since the combination of Champagne and berry-flavored liqueur is such an obvious success in the Kir Royale. Adding vodka gives a kick to that same seductive mix of bubbles and fruit flavors.

Add the vodka and raspberry liqueur to a cocktail shaker filled with cubed ice. Shake the contents to chill the drink and fine strain into a cocktail glass. Top with Champagne and serve.

Plenty of other fruit liqueurs can be used in the Metropolis to replace the raspberry chosen here. Tried-and-tested alternatives include peach, blackcurrant, grapefruit, and elderflower.

James Bond

The James Bond is a variation on the elegant Champagne Cocktail, using vodka instead of the more traditional brandy. The naming of this cocktail is a mystery since the eponymous spy liked his drinks shaken not stirred, as in this cocktail.

1 white sugar cube
2 dashes of Angostura bitters
1 part vodka
Champagne, to top up

Place the sugar cube in the bottom of a Champagne flute and add a couple of dashes of Angostura bitters—this will moisten the cube and impart some bitterness to balance the sweetness. Next, pour the vodka into the glass and top with Champagne.

The creation of the Moscow Mule dates back to 1940s New York and its popularity ensured that word of this glorious drink quickly spread to California and beyond. It's the drink that woke us up to the godsend that is ginger beer, which lends the Mule its legendary kick and an easy spiciness.

Moscow Mule

2 parts vodka
½ part lime juice
Ginger beer, to top up
Garnish: ½ lime,
cut into 3 wedges

GLASSWARE:

If you're a traditionalist, then you should serve this drink in a copper mug. If you don't have one of those to hand, a highball glass will do the job just as well. Start by filling your chosen glassware with cubed ice, then pour in the vodka and the lime juice. Top up the glass with ginger beer and stir gently with a barspoon. To finish, garnish with the lime wedges.

Strawberry Mule

2 thin fresh ginger slices
3 fresh strawberries
2 parts vodka
½ part strawberry liqueur
Dash of simple syrup (see page 23)
Ginger beer, to top up
Garnish: A strawberry, cut into quarters

There are many takes on the basic mule formula, here is one that is perfect for an afternoon in the sun. The extra addition of sliced fresh ginger gives a welcome fieriness to the drink and who could resist the lure of strawberries on a gorgeous summer day? If your drinks cupboard is lacking a bottle of vodka, don't panic. Try substituting dark rum or bourbon for the vodka for a delicious alternative.

GLASSWARE:

Start by adding the two slices of ginger into a cocktail shaker along with three strawberries. Muddle these ingredients together until you have a purée. Next, add the vodka, strawberry liqueur, and simple syrup and shake all the ingredients together—no ice is needed here. Use a fine strainer to remove any strawberry seeds or shreds of ginger and pour the liquid into a highball glass filled with ice. To finish, top up the glass with ginger beer, add your strawberry quarters, and give it a gentle stir. Serve with two straws.

Black Russian

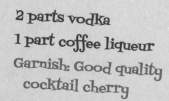

2 parts vodka
1 part coffee liqueur
Garnish: Good quality
cocktail cherry

GLASSWARE:

The Black and White Russians are classics that have been on the scene for many years. The black version was first to arrive on the cocktail scene, with a Belgian barman Gustave Tops credited as the inventor, making the drink for the US ambassador for Luxembourg in 1949. The white version came into being a decade or so later, when fresh cream was added into the mix. Both drinks make stylish after-dinner cocktails with their sweet coffee flavor, which is sharpened up by the vodka... Russian vodka, of course.

Add both the ingredients to a cocktail shaker filled with cubed ice. Shake for around 15 seconds to chill and strain into a rocks glass filled with ice. Garnish with a stemmed cherry.

White Russian

2 parts vodka
1 part coffee liqueur
1 part single/light cream
Garnish: Good quality
cocktail cherry

The White Russian, with its addition of cream, retains a cult following thanks to its position as the preferred tipple of uber-slacker the Dude in the Coen Brothers' film The Big Lebowski. Chances are you'll come across people dressed in bath robes drinking White Russians at many Halloween parties. Why not join these dudes by making your own, just be sure not to spill any on the rug!

There are two options to turn the Black Russian White. The first and simplest method is to add all the ingredients into a cocktail shaker filled with ice, shake, and strain the liquid into a rocks glass packed with ice. For a more interesting-looking version, start by following the method listed opposite for the Black Russian. Once that's done, layer the cream into the glass over the back of a barspoon. You don't have to be too precise, a bit of white cream bleeding into the black liquid can look pretty cool. For both versions, garnish with a stemmed cherry.

Vodka Espresso

1 part espresso coffee
2 parts vodka
1 part simple syrup (see page 23)
Garnish: 2 or 3 coffee beans

GLASSWARE:

If there was ever a yin and yang of cocktails this one is it. With its dark velvety body and creamy top, the Vodka Espresso was designed both to wake up and to calm down its recipient simultaneously. It's an excellent choice for a first drink pick-me-up following a long day at the office, with the caffeine providing a welcome energy boost and the alcohol helping you to relax.

First make your espresso. Once that's ready, pour it into a cocktail shaker and add the vodka and simple syrup. Quickly fill the shaker with ice cubes and shake the mixture hard for around 20 seconds to cool down the hot coffee and combine the ingredients. Once condensation appears on the outside of the shaker, strain the liquid into a chilled cocktail glass or alternatively pour into a rocks glass filled with ice cubes. A pretty head of foam should appear at the top of the cocktail on which you can place your coffee-bean garnish.

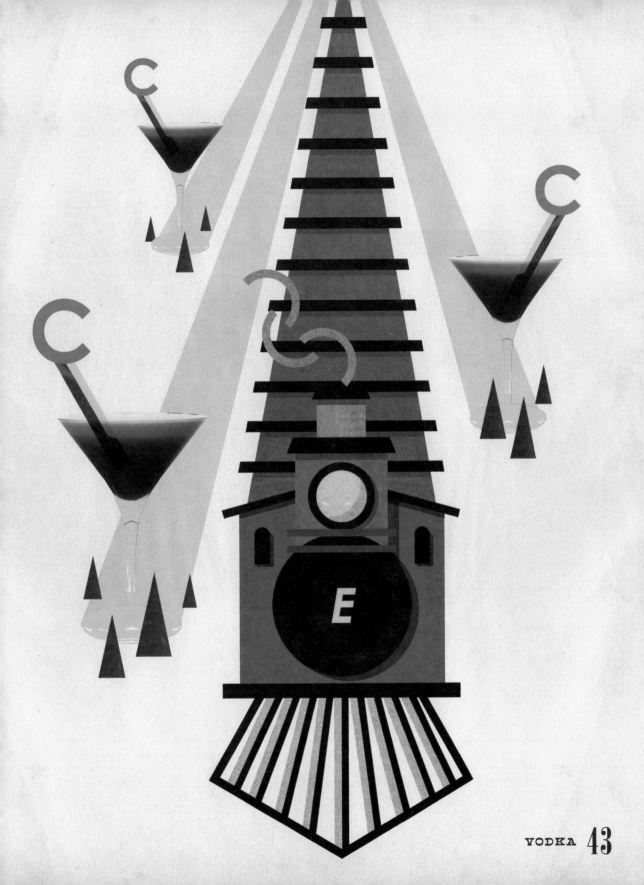

VODKA 43

Mandarin Caipiroska

This twist on the Caipiroska switches the limes for mandarins—a traditionally winter fruit but one that is now available most of the year. It's a good job too, because this is actually the perfect summertime barbecue cocktail, working really well with smoky grilled food.

1 mandarin, cut into wedges
Fresh mint leaves
1 part orange liqueur
1 part vodka
Tonic water, to top up
Garnish: Mint sprig

This is a drink that can be assembled in the glass. Drop the mandarin wedges and mint leaves into a highball glass, squeezing the wedges as you go to release the juices. Pour over the orange liqueur and vodka, then top up with tonic water to serve. Garnish with a mint sprig.

Don't worry if you can't find any mandarins at your local supermarket. Tangerines or even oranges can make a perfectly serviceable substitute.

Claret Cobbler

Once deemed to be "without doubt the most popular beverage in the country" by renowned American bartender Harry Johnson, the venerable cobbler was all the rage during the second half of the nineteenth century. Traditionally the drink was commonly a mix of sugar, fruit, and fortified wines like sherry, but below the recipe has been tweaked to add a shot of vodka to up the booze levels.

1 lemon slice

1 lime wedge

1 orange wheel

1¼ parts claret or port

1 part vodka

1 part raspberry liqueur

Garnish: Lemon and orange wheels

Start by putting all three citrus fruits in a cocktail shaker and muddle together to release the juices. Next, add the liquid ingredients to the shaker along with some cubed ice. Give the contents a decent shake and strain through a sieve into a highball glass filled with ice. To finish, garnish with a lemon and an orange wheel.

Choose red Bordeaux or Cabernet-Merlot blends for the claret.

Sea Breeze

GLASSWARE:

1½ parts fresh pink grapefruit juice
3 parts cranberry juice
1 part vodka
½ a lime, cut into wedges
Garnish: Lime wedge

With a name that's so evocative of days sat on the beach, you just know that the Sea Breeze is going to be made for summer drinking. Not only is it one of the easiest cocktails to put together, but it's also a really easy drinker that can make you feel pleasantly sleepy. Be sure to put on a decent amount of sunscreen—no-one wants to wake up looking like a lobster having necked one too many of these.

Pour the pink grapefruit juice, cranberry juice, and vodka into a cocktail shaker filled with cubed ice. Squeeze the juice from a couple of lime wedges into the shaker as well. Give the contents a good, firm shake and strain into a highball glass filled with ice. Add a lime wedge as a garnish before serving.

Vodka Collins

While Tom was first on the scene way back in the nineteenth century, the Vodka Collins, or Joe Collins as it's sometimes referred to, is an enormously popular twist on its big brother. Sharp, zingy, and thirst quenching, this drink is so good it's easy to forget there is any alcohol in it!

GLASSWARE:

2½ parts vodka
1 part fresh lemon juice
¾ part simple syrup
(see page 23)
Soda water, to top up
Garnish: Lemon slice

Fill a highball glass with ice cubes and add the vodka, lemon juice, and simple syrup. Top up the rest of the glass with soda water and give everything a gentle stir before garnishing the drink with a slice of lemon and a couple of straws. If you're feeling fancy, some drinkers shake the first three ingredients with ice to chill before pouring into the highball glass, but really it's just going to mean more washing up.

Peach Rickey

A Peach Rickey is a fantastic summer cooler and the perfect way to use up a surplus of juicy peaches. Ripe peaches will yield the best results if you're making your own purée, and you should because it's really easy to do. Simply blitz the peaches until smooth in a food processor and you're ready to go. Be sure to save a segment of the peach to use later as a garnish.

2½ parts vodka
1 part fresh lime juice
Dash of peach liqueur or peach schnapps
¾ part peach purée
Soda water, to top up
Garnish: Peach slice or fan

Fill a highball glass with ice cubes and add in the vodka, lime juice, peach liqueur, and peach purée. Top up the glass with the soda water and give the contents a gentle stir to mix all the ingredients together. Add a thin slice or fan of fresh peach to garnish and you are good to go.

Godchild

GLASSWARE: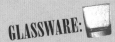

1 part vodka
1 part Amaretto
1 part double/heavy cream
Garnish: Grated nutmeg
(optional)

Here's a riff on the Godfather cocktail—a mix of Scotch whisky and Amaretto that was rumored to be a favorite of the actor Marlon Brando. For this version, vodka replaces the Scotch and cream is added to make it the perfect after-dinner tipple. You can also try serving this one long with milk for a less intense flavor. Grate some fresh nutmeg over the surface of the drink to add a whole new depth of taste.

Fill a cocktail shaker with cubed ice and add in the the vodka, Ameretto, and cream. Give the ingredients a good shake for around 15 seconds and fine strain into into a rocks glass filled with ice cubes. Some freshly grated nutmeg is an excellent finishing touch if you have some to hand (the pre-ground version is OK to use as well).

Cosmopolitan

With '90s nostalgia currently in full swing here's a drink that every self-respecting bartender was serving back when drinkers played snake on their Nokias while waiting for friends to turn up at the bar, Sex and the City was the top-rated show, and Alanis Morrisette blared out of every stereo. For some proper '90s flair bartending you can flame the orange peel.

Pour the vodka, orange liqueur, lime juice, and cranberry juice into a cocktail shaker filled with cubed ice. Give the contents a good shake to chill everything down and fine strain into a pre-chilled cocktail glass. To finish, squeeze the peel (with or without flame— see below) over the glass, rub the peel around the rim, and place in the drink.

2 parts citrus vodka
¾ part orange liqueur
¾ part fresh lime juice
1 part cranberry juice
Garnish: Orange Peel (flamed if you're feeling brave)

HOW TO FLAME ORANGE PEEL

It's debatable how much impact this little trick has to the flavor of your drink, but what is undeniable is it certainly looks cool and after a few practices you'll be flaming like a pro. Start by cutting a piece of citrus peel (oranges and lemons work the best) roughly 1-inch (2.5-cm) square. Next, hold a lighter or a lit match in one hand over your cocktail and in the other squeeze the peel (with the skin facing the flame) sharply over the flame. A tip: the fresher the fruit the more oils present in the skin and more impressive pyrotechnics.

Ginger Cosmo

For a really simple variation on the classic Cosmopolitan (see page 52), try adding some fresh ginger. The mix of orange zest, lime juice, and lemon vodka with the pungent ginger gives this drink an incredible depth of taste.

2 parts citrus vodka
¾ part orange liqueur
¾ part fresh lime juice
1 part cranberry juice
2 thin fresh ginger slices
Garnish: orange peel or twist

GLASSWARE:

Start by muddling the ginger slices in a cocktail shaker. Next, add in the vodka, orange liqueur, lime juice, and cranberry juice along with a handful or two of ice cubes. Shake the ingredients for at least 10 seconds and fine strain the liquid into a chilled cocktail glass. As with the Cosmopolitan, garnish with an orange twist or peel—flamed or otherwise (see page 52).

Cosmo Iced Tea

GLASSWARE:

2 parts vanilla vodka
1 part orange liqueur
5½ parts cranberry juice
1 part fresh lime juice
Garnish: Lime wedge

Not quite as in your face as the classic Cosmopolitan, this version is served long rather than straight up. By upping the amount of cranberry juice, the cocktail gains a fruity, refreshing quality, which is softened by the orange liqueur. The vanilla vodka adds a final element of sweetness to round the drink off beautifully.

Fill a cocktail shaker with cubed ice and add in all the liquid ingredients. Give everything a firm shake for around 15 seconds before straining into a standard highball glass half-filled with ice cubes. To finish, add a lime wedge to the rim and serve with a straw or two.

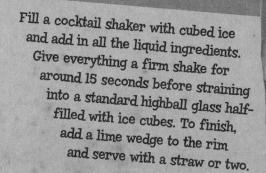

Cosmo Royale

If you thought sipping Cosmopolitans in elegant cocktail bars was the height of sophistication then you clearly haven't tried the Cosmo Royale. This takes the original and pimps it with the decadent inclusion of a Champagne float. How fabulous does that sound? Definitely not as fabulous as it actually tastes!

2 parts citrus vodka
1 part fresh lime juice
1 part orange liqueur
3 parts cranberry juice
Champagne, to top up
Garnish: orange twist

GLASSWARE:

Take a cocktail shaker and carefully measure in the citrus vodka, lime juice, orange liqueur, and cranberry juice. Fill the shaker with cubed ice and give everything a firm shake. Strain the liquid into a chilled Champagne glass and very carefully top up with Champagne. To finish, garnish with an orange twist.

1½ parts raspberry vodka

1 part raspberry syrup
   (see page 82)

¾ part lemon juice

1 egg white

Garnish: Raspberry on a
   cocktail stick/toothpick

Raspberry Sour

GLASSWARE:

If there's one cocktail recipe you should commit to memory it's for the sour. Using a ratio of 6:4:3—with 6 being for the base spirit, 4 for the sweet ingredient, and 3 for the sour ingredient— you can make a host of different drinks such as the Margarita or Daiquiri. Here the ratio has been used to make a vodka sour that's a tip of the hat to the Clover Club (see page 82) thanks to the raspberry-infused vodka and the egg white foam.

Add the vodka, syrup, and lemon juice to a cocktail shaker along with the egg white. Don't add any ice! You want to dry shake the ingredients first in order to allow the egg white to emulsify at room temperature and produce a thicker foam. After the dry shake, add some cubed ice and shake until condensation appears on the outside of the shaker. Fine strain the liquid into a cocktail glass and garnish with a raspberry on a cocktail stick/toothpick.

Chili Martini

Here's a drink that brings pleasure and pain in equal measures, making it a must-try for anyone who appreciates the endorphin rush that fiery chili peppers bring. The chili-infused vodka can be as potent as you like depending on the length of the infusion and the strength of the chilis you choose—habaneros and scotch bonnets are pretty punchy so tread carefully. You can also buy pre-infused versions like 250,000 Scovilles Naga Chili Vodka, made from the world's hottest pepper, the naga jalokia.

Add the infused vodka to a mixing glass filled with ice and stir until the glass is frosted. This part offers an important element of dilution to the vodka, making it easier to drink. Strain the vodka into a chilled cocktail glass to remove the ice and garnish with a chili on the rim.

CHILI-INFUSED VODKA

Place three chilies (with seeds) into a bottle of vodka and leave until they start to lose their color—the more translucent the chilies become, the more flavor has been absorbed into the vodka. (This will take a few days.)

2 parts chili-infused vodka (see box)

Garnish: Whole chili

1 part zubrowka vodka
1 part honey liqueur
1 part fresh apple juice
Garnish: Apple fan

Polish Martini

GLASSWARE:

This twist on the Martini takes the edge off the alcohol with the addition of honey liqueur—the most readily available brand being Krupnik. Zubrowka, a herbal vodka flavored with bison grass is used here, the bitterness of which balances the potent sweetness of the liqueur and combines with the crispness of apple juice to create a beguiling depth of taste.

Stirring is the key here rather than shaking. Start by filling a mixing glass with the vodka, liqueur, and apple juice. Next, add a good handful of ice cubes and stir for around 15 seconds. Strain into a chilled cocktail glass and garnish with an apple fan.

Black Bison

Since you've bought your Zubrowka to make the Polish Martini on page 59, it'd be rude not to give you another recipe to try. The vodka plays a key role, adding its distinctly herbal characteristics to the mix, working excellently with the sweet sharpness of hedgerow fruit brought by the fresh blackcurrants and blackberry liqueur.

4 fresh blackcurrants
2 parts zubrowka vodka
1¼ parts blackberry liqueur
½ part fresh lime juice
Dash of simple syrup
(see page 23)
Garnish: A blueberry

GLASSWARE:

Place the blackcurrants in a cocktail shaker and muddle to release the juices. Pour in the Zubrowka, blackberry liqueur, lime juice, and a dash of simple syrup then top up the shaker with some ice cubes. Give all the ingredients a good, hard shake before fine straining into a chilled cocktail glass. To finish, garnish with a blueberry, ideally skewered on a cocktail stick/toothpick.

BC BANNED IN DC

Until recently, blackcurrants were considered forbidden fruit in the US and were banned across the land as they were considered a danger to the logging industry. In recent years that federal ban has been overturned and the currants are once again available in many states, but Maine, New Hampshire, Virginia, and Massachusetts still have it in for these innocent little berries.

Tatanka

Here's a cocktail that is so easy to make, using the herbal, hay flavors of the Zubrowka and combining them with refreshing, fruity apple juice. It's worth investing in some good-quality pressed apple juice here rather than the cheaper stuff made from concentrate. The latter might make for a prettier, clearer drink but the taste just can't compare to the cloudier version.

2 parts zubrowka vodka
3 parts cloudy apple juice
Garnish: Cinnamon stick

This is super quick to make—simply pour the ingredients straight into a highball glass filled with ice. Pop in a cinnamon stick garnish to stir everything up and you're good to go.

This one's for the party animals and glamorpusses looking to stay out until the early hours. Here the clubber's classic Red Bull and Vodka gets a makeover, turning it into something a little more refined thanks to the addition of Champagne or other sparkling wine of your choice. This fizzy little tipple is guaranteed to kick-start any big night out and keep you going until sunrise!

1 part citron vodka
3 parts Champagne or sparkling wine
3 parts Red Bull or energy drink of your choice
Garnish: orange slice and mint sprig (both optional)

GLASSWARE:

Hollywood Hustle

To start, fill up a tumbler or rocks glass with crushed ice and pour over the citron vodka. Next, pour in the Champagne and Red Bull in equal measures and you are ready to serve. For a more attractive glass, garnish with an orange slice, a sprig of mint, and a couple of straws.

Metropolitan

Here's another drink that was big in the '90s, this time cropping up on the menu of the London cocktail haunt the Met Bar. This was a place where the great and the not-so-good of the Cool Britannia movement went to let their hair down, having slathered themselves in CK One perfume and danced in the mirror to Oasis before leaving the house. It's a simple yet devastatingly effective twist on the Cosmo. The blackcurrant vodka, combined with the cranberry and lime juices makes for quite a fruity concoction.

2 parts blackcurrant vodka
1 part orange liqueur
1 part fresh lime juice
1 part cranberry juice
Garnish: orange zest

Add all the ingredients to a cocktail shaker filled with ice. Shake sharply and strain into a frosted cocktail glass. To finish, flame a strip of orange zest over the glass (see page 52). Rub the rim with the burnt orange zest before dropping it into the cocktail.

Tropical Breeze

A breeze is a cocktail that contains a spirit (traditionally vodka), cranberry juice, and then one other fruit juice. The original version is the Sea Breeze, which chooses grapefruit as the third component. Here the recipe is tweaked to include melon vodka, but try any flavored vodka lurking in your cocktail cabinet—raspberry, citrus, grapefruit, blackcurrant, pear, and apple flavors would all make excellent choices.

2 parts melon vodka
3 parts cranberry juice
3 parts fresh grapefruit juice
Garnish: Thin grapefruit slice or two

Pour the melon-flavored vodka into a highball glass filled with ice. Top with equal amounts of cranberry and fresh grapefruit juice. garnish with a slice or two of grapefruit and maybe a straw.

The beauty of this drink is that it's completely open to experimentation. Gin lovers might like to try a shot of that rather than the vodka or for a Caribbean twist, try rum and apple juice with the cranberry.

Mandarin Mule

2 parts mandarin vodka
½ part lime juice
½ part orange liqueur
5 parts ginger beer
Garnish: Lime wedge

GLASSWARE: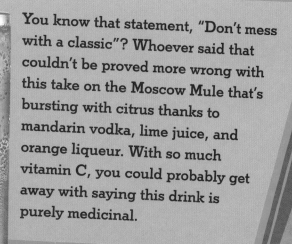

You know that statement, "Don't mess with a classic"? Whoever said that couldn't be proved more wrong with this take on the Moscow Mule that's bursting with citrus thanks to mandarin vodka, lime juice, and orange liqueur. With so much vitamin C, you could probably get away with saying this drink is purely medicinal.

Pour the mandarin vodka and the lime juice into a highball glass along with four or five cubes of ice. Next, add the orange liqueur and top up with the ginger beer, garnishing with a lime wedge.

Dry Martini

GLASSWARE:

6 parts gin
½–1½ parts dry vermouth
Garnish: Citrus peel or olive

Although the world's most popular cocktail is the Margarita (see page 108), the internationally recognized image for a cocktail is not this Mexican creation but the Dry Martini, presented in a V-shaped cocktail glass, garnished with an olive. The reasons are many:

✻ Few drinks allow the elegant consumption of virtually neat alcohol, and the huge number of variations inherent in the recipe allow for that most precious of commodities in our identikit world: personalization.

✻ A favorite gin, a particular vermouth, the ratio of these ingredients, and choice of garnish mean it's easy to make the Martini your own. The process of finding your perfect version can be arduous but very rewarding. Almost any gin will make a good Martini, but those over 50% ABV need a little more care, and an extra stir or two.

✻ The amount of vermouth used can be as little as Winston Churchill specified: "I would like to observe the vermouth from across the room while drinking my Martini," or, like the original drink, much wetter (more vermouth) with a recipe approaching two parts gin to one vermouth. Just remember that vermouth is a fortified, aromatized wine and will oxidize, altering the flavor. Keep vermouth in the refrigerator and don't be afraid to throw away an old bottle.

Martinis must be COLD! Each aspect of the method must be designed to produce the coldest drink possible, with the ideal serving temperature 19°F (-7°C). To achieve this, it is vital to keep the cocktail glass in the freezer until the last possible moment, making sure the garnish is ready and the drinker keen in anticipation.

Stir the chosen amounts of gin and vermouth together with cubed ice. Avoid using frozen gin because very little water is added from melting ice, and the drink will be too strong—to achieve the standard optimum of 28% ABV, a significant amount of water needs to be added. If you have a steel-walled (not glass) vacuum flask, stirring the drink inside will maximize the chilling effect of the ice and also allow for dilution—a digital thermometer is useful here to check that the correct temperature is reached.

Strain the drink into a frozen cocktail glass and garnish with citrus peel or olives, but remember that a warm garnish will undo all your good work in making a cold drink, so keep them in the refrigerator before adding or serve them on the side.

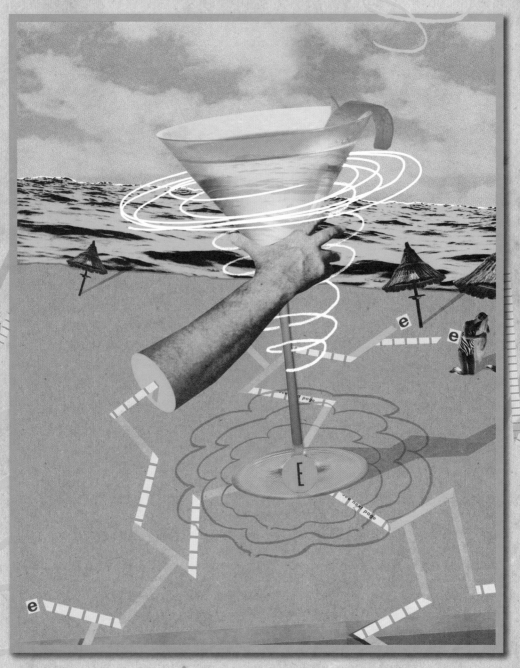

Gimlet

2 parts gin
1 part lime cordial
Garnish: 1 lime wedge
or twist

GLASSWARE:

Sharp yet sweet, the Gimlet is an excellent choice when the summer months come around. The cocktail's original recipes were made with equal parts gin to lime cordial, but to the modern palate this can be a little cloying. As a result, most Gimlets served today come with a higher gin content to increase the sharpness. The classic lime cordial to use is Rose's, which is readily available in most supermarkets.

Add the gin and lime cordial to a cocktail shaker filled with cubed ice. Shake the ingredients hard for around 15 seconds and fine strain into a chilled cocktail glass. Garnish with a lime wedge or twist on the rim of the glass.

Vesper

4 parts gin
1 part vodka
½ part dry vermouth
Garnish: Lemon peel

When one thinks of the Dry Martini, one immediately conjures up images of James Bond uttering the immortal line of "Shaken, not stirred." But the classic Martini is not the only version the British secret agent drank. In the 1953 novel Casino Royale, Bond asks a barman to amend the original by adding vodka into the mix. He renames the drink Vesper, naming it after the double agent Vesper Lynd.

GLASSWARE:

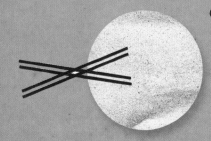

Given the wishes of the creator of the Vesper, this is a Martini that must be shaken. Add the ingredients to a cocktail shaker filled with cubed ice and shake hard until condensation appears on the outside of the tin. Fine strain the liquid into a cocktail glass to remove any shards of ice and garnish with a slice of lemon peel.

Created in 1915 at Harry's Bar in Paris, and so named because consuming it was considered reminiscent of being shelled with a 75mm artillery piece, this classic cocktail has aged very well. It can be made with any gin but some of the more modern, citrus-led examples produce a softer, finer beverage. The original calls for Champagne but it will happily work with your favorite dry sparkling wine.

French 75

3 parts gin
1½ parts lemon juice
1½ parts simple syrup
  (see page 23)
6 parts Champagne
Garnish: Lemon twist

GLASSWARE:

Pour the Champagne into a chilled Champagne flute. Put all the other ingredients into a cocktail shaker with cubed ice and shake. Pour gently over the Champagne, fine straining to remove any ice shards. Garnish with a lemon twist.

There is another story about the origins of this drink. It's said that during the French celebrations after the end of the German occupation in World War I, the few intact cellars remaining were cracked open and Cognac and Champagne were mixed. Regardless of the truth, a French 75 with Cognac is a beautiful thing.

5 parts gin
1 part dry vermouth
Dash of crème de cassis
Garnish: lemon zest (optional)

Graham Greene

This drink was created in the Metropole Hotel in Hanoi for its famous namesake author while he was writing The Quiet American in 1951. It breaks Dry Martini convention with a very sweet ingredient, crème de cassis, but the tart character of the blackcurrants pairs nicely with the dry vermouth to balance the drink. Due to the fruity nature of the liqueur, light floral gins work very well in this recipe.

GLASSWARE:

Stir all the ingredients with cubed ice and strain into a frozen cocktail glass. As with the Martini, you can be flexible with the measurements, but the drink should be pale pink in color, not purple. As crème de cassis will oxidize and go brown, losing the tart berry notes to a caramel sludge taste, it is often sensible to buy miniature bottles of it (and other fruit liqueurs) to ensure less potential wastage. Graham Greene took no garnish, but some lemon zest brings out more freshness and fruit.

Gibson

GLASSWARE:

6 parts gin
1 part dry vermouth
Garnish: Pickled
silverskin onions

The Gibson is the most famous variation on a Martini and differs only in the garnish and the specific ratio of ingredients. Cornichon gherkins, sun-dried tomatoes wrapped in Parma ham, asparagus spears, and a thousand other savory delights make the perfect counterpoint to an ice-cold Gibson.

Stir the gin and vermouth together over cubed ice, aiming to add 1oz (25ml) of water through dilution, and strain into a frozen cocktail glass. Garnish with at least one pickled silverskin onion on a cocktail stick/toothpick. For elegance and taste, try to find small, smooth-skinned pickled onions and limit the amount of pickling liquor transferred to the glass. When in doubt, serve the onions on the side—ideally, the number should be the same as the number of sips taken to consume the drink.

Golden Gibson

Tastes have become steadily drier over the years, and the proportion of vermouth in martinis has declined accordingly. This drink is a throwback to wet martinis, old tom gin, and Liebfraumilch wine. Slightly sweet, it needs to be cold, but the herbaceous sweetness that contrasts with the spicy vinegar bite of the marinated onions is a thing of beauty. Always have extra onions on standby! Try this with your favorite gin, or perhaps even vodka.

6 parts gin
1 part Benedictine
Garnish: 2 infused onions (see box)

Stir the gin and Benedictine together in the style of a Dry Martini and strain into a chilled cocktail glass. Garnish with a pair of infused onions on a cocktail stick/toothpick

GLASSWARE:

Pickled onions are available in many sizes—for cocktails, the ideal size is ½ in (1.5cm) across. To infuse a 12oz (350g) jar of pickled onions, you will need to add 1 tbsp brown sugar, 1 tsp ground turmeric, and 4 stamens of saffron, then leave for, ideally, 72 hours.

Wibble

Created by the UK's most famous bartender, Dick Bradsell, with the tag line: "A Wibble. It might make you wobble but you won't fall over." Sloe gin is technically a liqueur, made by steeping the fruits of the blackthorn (sloes) in gin with equal parts sugar and letting it infuse for many months. The fruit is then removed and the liqueur can be used. The Wibble brings a complex blend of flavors, but is beautifully balanced.

2½ parts gin
2½ parts sloe gin
2½ parts pink grapefruit juice
1 part simple syrup (see page 23)
1 part lemon juice
1 part crème de mûre
Garnish: Lemon twist

Shake all the ingredients in a cocktail shaker with cubed ice and strain into a chilled cocktail glass. Garnish with a lemon twist.

Southside

Although created in New York, this drink became famed in Chicago, where a version made with crushed ice, similar in style to a Mojito, was drunk during Prohibition by mobsters from the south side of the city. Their competitors from the northern boroughs had to suffer the much less palatable Northside, a mix of gin and ginger ale.

The original Southside is served straight up but feel free to try the gangster version. It also forms the basis of the Southside Fizz, served over ice with a spritz of soda water, and the Southside Royale, topped with Champagne. Lighter gins work best here, as the combination of heavy juniper notes and mint can taste a little medicinal.

5 parts gin
2 parts lime juice
2 parts simple syrup
(see page 23)
6 mint leaves
Garnish: Small mint leaf

Shake all the ingredients in a cocktail shaker with ice cubes and strain into a chilled cocktail glass. Use a fine strainer to remove any small flecks of mint. Garnish with a small mint leaf.

2 parts honey syrup
5 parts gin
2 parts lemon juice
Garnish: Lemon zest

Bees Knees

GLASSWARE:

Honey is a fantastic cocktail ingredient. It's cheap and, due to its intense concentration of sugars, has a virtually indefinite shelf life. Unfortunately, its viscosity is profoundly affected by temperature—as soon as it begins to chill, it becomes too thick to incorporate with other ingredients and sticks to the shaker. To use it effectively, it needs to be relaxed with a little water and made into a syrup. You can experiment with different wild flower honeys to pair with your chosen gin— orange blossom honey works well with gin that contains orange as a botanical, and you can make a delicious variation of the Bees Knees by adding two parts freshly squeezed orange juice.

Add all the ingredients to a cocktail shaker along with a good handful of cubed ice. Shake hard and strain into a chilled cocktail glass. Garnish with a slice of lemon zest.

To make the honey syrup, mix three parts runny honey with one part hot water and stir until fully amalgamated and let cool. This syrup will keep for about a week in the refrigerator.

Created by Dick Bradsell in London, originally with Bombay Sapphire gin, the Bramble is widely regarded as one of the best cocktails of the dire cocktail decade of the 1980s. It uses crème de mûre, a liqueur made from blackberries, but a good framboise or cassis will make a great variation. Don't feel limited to Bombay Sapphire—although it works well, all but the heaviest gins will make a delicious Bramble.

5 parts gin
2½ parts lemon juice
1 part simple syrup
(see page 23)
2 parts crème de mûre
Garnish: Lemon slice
and mint sprig

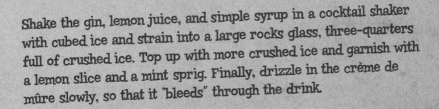

Bramble

GLASSWARE:

Shake the gin, lemon juice, and simple syrup in a cocktail shaker with cubed ice and strain into a large rocks glass, three-quarters full of crushed ice. Top up with more crushed ice and garnish with a lemon slice and a mint sprig. Finally, drizzle in the crème de mûre slowly, so that it "bleeds" through the drink.

Albion

5 parts gin
2 parts lemon juice
1 part simple syrup
(see page 23)
1 tbsp morello cherry
preserve
½ egg white
Garnish: Fresh cherries
(optional)

GLASSWARE:

Cocktail cherries are an abomination—they can't even be classed as food due to their harmful ingredients, so can only be described as a "food decoration." However, fresh cherries, jams, and liqueurs are wonderful cocktail ingredients. You can make this recipe by finely chopping six seeded cherries and shaking them into the drink. I recommend a full-bodied spicy gin to balance with the rich cherry flavor.

Put all the ingredients into a cocktail shaker and shake, without ice, to incorporate air into the egg white. Add cubed ice to the shaker and shake hard, then strain the mix into a chilled coupette or cocktail glass, making sure to include all the creamy head. This cocktail needs no garnish but if cherries are in season, it would be churlish not to add one or two.

Morello cherry preserve normally has a relatively liquid consistency, but if yours is very set, it might be worth relaxing it a little with some boiling water, so that it mixes more effectively.

Space Gin Smash

Created by master bartender Pete Kendall at Trailer Happiness in London, the Space Gin Smash has been consistently the best-selling drink on every menu where it has appeared. The crowd-pleasing ingredients are in in perfect balance and suitable for any occasion, which makes it stunningly easy to have not just one or two Smashes, but one or two too many. It really is a true modern classic. Any gin will work here, from Hendrick's to Tanqueray, so experiment at will.

5 parts gin
2 parts apple juice
1½ parts elderflower cordial
1 part simple syrup (see page 23)
5 red grapes
5 mint leaves
3 lemon wedges
Garnish: Mint sprig, lemon wedge, red grapes

There are a couple of ways to make this drink. The original recipe calls for the grapes and the lemon wedges to be muddled first, with the other ingredients then added and swizzled with crushed ice. This tastes delicious but can look a bit "rustic."

For a prettier drink, muddle all the ingredients in the shaker, and shake and strain over cubed ice. Don't be tempted to substitute the lemon wedges for lemon juice, though—the oils extracted during muddling are a vital ingredient. Garnish with a mint sprig, lemon wedge, and a grape or two.

GLASSWARE:

Clover Club

As with many classic cocktails, there are arguments over the Clover Club's creation and its recipe—some omit the dry vermouth entirely while others call for a dash of sweet vermouth in addition or instead. Certainly, the drink has been popular since the 1930s and is still universally well received today.

1½ parts raspberry syrup (see box)

4½ parts gin

1½ parts dry vermouth

2 parts lemon juice

½ egg white

Shake all the ingredients in a cocktail shaker without ice to emulsify the egg white. Add cubed ice and shake until the liquid is cooled. Strain into a chilled large cocktail glass.

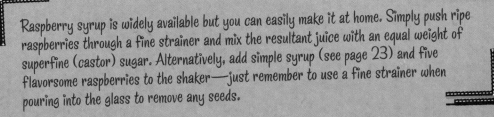

Raspberry syrup is widely available but you can easily make it at home. Simply push ripe raspberries through a fine strainer and mix the resultant juice with an equal weight of superfine (castor) sugar. Alternatively, add simple syrup (see page 23) and five flavorsome raspberries to the shaker—just remember to use a fine strainer when pouring into the glass to remove any seeds.

2½ parts gin
2½ parts sloe gin
2 parts lemon juice
1 part simple syrup (see page 23)
5 parts soda water
1½ parts crème de mûre
Garnish: Lemon slice,
    blackberry, and raspberry

GLASSWARE:

Hedgerow Sling

Possibly the most delicious Collins recipe ever made, the Hedgerow Sling has it all: complexity of flavor but still refreshing, a suitable size that should last for a while, and very pretty to boot. The drink relies on the best ingredients and stands tall as is, but if you are able to get hold of good-quality ripe fall fruits, such as raspberries, blackberries, or redcurrants, it is worth throwing a couple into the shaker for that extra dimension. Try with a classic London dry gin like Beefeater.

Shake all the ingredients in a cocktail shaker, except for the soda water and crème de mûre, and strain over cubed ice into a sling glass. Add a little crushed ice and top with soda water. As a final touch, slowly drizzle the crème de mûre over the top, so that it "bleeds" down through the drink. Garnish with a lemon slice and a berry or two.

White Lady

Putatively created in 1930 by Harry Craddock at the American Bar at the Savoy Hotel in London for the fabulously named Zelda Sayre Fitzgerald, wife of F. Scott Fitzgerald, this cocktail is elevated from the simple, daisy-style drink by the addition of egg white. This changes both the color and texture to that of a delicious citrus cloud. Almost any gin will work in this recipe, but avoid anything above 50% ABV.

4 parts gin
2 parts orange liqueur
2 parts lemon juice
½ part simple syrup
(see page 23)
½ egg white
Garnish: Large orange
or lemon twist

Place all the ingredients in a cocktail shaker and shake without ice to start frothing the egg white. Add cubed ice, shake hard, and strain into a chilled cocktail glass. Garnish with a large orange or lemon twist

GLASSWARE:

Ramos Fizz

5 parts gin
1 part lemon juice
1 part lime juice
2 parts simple syrup (see page 23)
2 parts single cream
1 egg white
orange flower water (see box)
Soda water, to top up

GLASSWARE: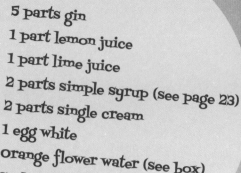

One of the few classic cocktails with a history beyond dispute, the Ramos Fizz was created in 1888 by Henry C. Ramos in New Orleans and originally called the New Orleans Fizz. Ramos kept the recipe a secret and also feared his drink would die with the advent of Prohibition, but following his death in 1928, Ramos' brother posthumously released the recipe in his honor.

The original Ramos Fizz called for a 12-minute shake undertaken by a team of bartenders, with each one passing on the shaker to the next when exhausted. The drink can still be made that way, if you have a mind, but it does lend itself to batch processing, particularly for parties, where the mixture is blended in a shaker without ice and then individual portions are shaken when needed for a more sensible amount of time.

Otherwise, simply shake all the ingredients, except the soda water, without ice for a LONG time—at least a few minutes—getting others to help if possible. Add some ice cubes and shake briefly to chill. Strain the contents into a chilled highball glass with no ice, then gently top with soda water. With the correct consistency, the head should stand proud of the rim and be stiff enough to hold a straw vertically.

Orange flower water is very pungent and varies in intensity from brand to brand. The first time you make a Ramos Fizz be very careful with the initial dose— it is easy to add more but impossible to take any out. Add a drop at a time.

2½ parts gin
2½ parts Campari
2½ parts sweet vermouth
Garnish: orange slice

Negroni

GLASSWARE:

The Negroni takes its name from Count Camillo Negroni, an habitué of the Casoni bar in Florence, just after World War I. After a bad day, the Count asked the bartender for his favored Americano cocktail, but "with a bit more kick." The bartender added a slug of gin, the Count was impressed, and very soon other patrons would call for Negroni's drink.

This cocktail is all about balance—the standard recipe calls for equal parts of all the ingredients, but don't be afraid to adjust them for personal preference. If you find Campari too bitter, reduce the amount used, and feel free to experiment with different styles of gin and sweet vermouth.

Stir all the ingredients with cubed ice in a large rocks glass, and garnish with a slice of orange.

New Cross Negroni

Created for the first menu at Meateasy, the birthplace of the British street food revolution, in London's New Cross, this drink was designed as a response to the burgeoning popularity of the Negroni and the fact that many found it a bit too much. This version has an altered emphasis, using a richer vermouth, Antica Formula, and a lighter aperitivo, Aperol, which is slightly more citrusy than Campari, with pronounced orange notes. It is also significantly less bitter. Although the original cocktail was made with Tanqueray, any good gin will work nicely. Other vermouth options include Dolin, Noilly Rouge, or Lillet Rouge (not technically a vermouth but it does make a mean Negroni).

2½ parts gin
2½ parts Aperol
2½ parts Carpano Antica Formula

Garnish: Large orange twist

Stir all the ingredients with cubed ice in a large rocks glass, and garnish with a large orange twist.

4 parts gin
1 part Cointreau
2 parts lemon juice
1 part simple syrup (see page 23)
½ egg white
1 scoop lemon sorbet
Garnish: Grated lemon zest,
silver spoon

This drink has its roots in the White Lady (see page 84), a classic mix of gin and Cointreau with fresh lemon. The addition of the lemon sorbet brings an extra texture and a bit of fun, making this a great party drink. It also works very well as a palate cleanser at a dinner party—simply halve the quantities and serve in smaller glasses.

Snow Angel

GLASSWARE:

Put all the ingredients, apart from the sorbet, into the cocktail shaker and shake hard, without ice, to start to emulsify the egg white. Fill the shaker with cubed ice and shake again. Strain into a chilled coupette or cocktail glass and place a scoop of sorbet in the center of the glass. Garnish with grated lemon zest and a spoon.

Lemon sorbet is widely available but it's very easy to make at home by heating lemon zest, superfine (castor) sugar, water, and lemon juice together, then freezing it in an ice-cream maker. You can also make the sorbet by hand by placing the mix in the freezer and removing it periodically to whisk. However, it is difficult to get the correct texture this way.

Soul Summer Cup

GLASSWARE:

2½ parts gin
2 parts Campari
2 parts sweet vermouth
1 part Cointreau
3 parts lemon juice
3 parts simple syrup (see page 23)
15 parts soda water

Garnish: Slices of orange, lemon, cucumber, and strawberries

Pimm's is a UK institution—hordes of people will be seen clutching pitchers of it on any available grassed surface as soon as you don't need a winter coat to be outside. Although delicious, it lacks a bit of character, so the store cupboard recipe below has a little extra alcohol and loads more flavor. Any traditional London dry gin will do, but for afternoon drinking, try to stick to one at 40% ABV.

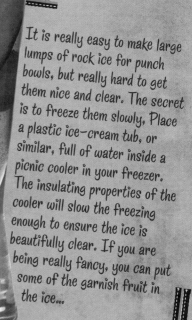

There are two methods for preparing this drink. For a single drink, it is worth taking the time to artfully arrange the myriad garnish ingredients. Start by putting cubed ice, a cucumber ribbon (or slices), and several slices of citrus fruit into a large highball glass. Add the remaining ingredients, stir, and top with more fruit.

For a group drink, multiply the ingredients by eight or ten, throw all the ingredients, along with the garnish, into a big punch bowl and add a large lump of rock ice (see box). Provide a ladle and some glasses, and invite your guests to do the work.

It is really easy to make large lumps of rock ice for punch bowls, but really hard to get them nice and clear. The secret is to freeze them slowly. Place a plastic ice-cream tub, or similar, full of water inside a picnic cooler in your freezer. The insulating properties of the cooler will slow the freezing enough to ensure the ice is beautifully clear. If you are being really fancy, you can put some of the garnish fruit in the ice...

Forbidden Aperitif

1 part gin
1 part Aperol
1 part lemon juice
1½ parts simple syrup
(see page 23)
5 parts sparkling wine
3 lemon verbena leaves
Garnish: small lemon twist

Hailing from South America, lemon verbena produces a strong lemon scent when bruised, which matches well with the floral notes of a light citrusy gin and the bitterness of Aperol, and is enlivened by the sparkling wine. There is no need to use the finest champagne here—a cava or other traditional méthode champenoise sparkling wine would be fine.

GLASSWARE:

If no fresh verbena is available, you can make a syrup from the dried herb. Simply soak ¼oz (7g/4 tbsp) in 1¼ cups (300ml) boiling water and let infuse for 3 minutes. Fine strain to remove the leaves, then mix with 1½ cups (300g) superfine (castor) sugar. Stir until the sugar is dissolved and let cool. The syrup can then be used in the recipe in place of the simple syrup.

Gently bruise the lemon verbena leaves with a muddler—you don't need to crush them too much, just enough to start releasing the aroma. Pour the sparkling wine into a chilled Champagne flute. Shake the remaining ingredients together in a cocktail shaker and fine strain into the glass—this will allow the ingredients to mix together more easily and reduce the amount of fizz.

Garnishing a Champagne flute can be difficult, as the glass is so narrow, but a small lemon twist, expressed by folding in half to release oils, does add another dimension to this drink.

Gin and Tonic

GLASSWARE:

2oz (50ml) gin
Tonic water, to top up
Garnish: Lime or lemon wedge

"Everyone knows how to make a G and T," you may cry, but just because it's so simple and ubiquitous doesn't mean there's no room for error. By observing a few key rules, this drink can be elevated to something absolutely outstanding:

* The drink should be served ice cold, so keep the tonic in the fridge and the ice in the freezer until the last moment.

* Pick your garnish according to the character of the gin. Some people swear by the bold citrus flavor of limes, while others prefer the gentler lemon; try both and see what works best for you. Some gins use cucumber, grapefruit, or even strawberries, but generally you can't go wrong with either lemon or lime.

* Don't scrimp on the gin, you should have at least 2oz (50ml). You want a decent measure to be able to taste the alcohol, with the botanicals in the spirit working their magic alongside those in the tonic.

* Pay attention to tonics—this ingredient makes up most of the glass so try different tonics until you find your perfect combination. With tonic, it's a good idea to use small, individual-serve bottles rather than larger plastic bottles, otherwise the tonic is in danger of going flat.

* Try adding a flavored liqueur. A dash of sloe gin or elderflower liqueur is an excellent choice.

Start by preparing your chosen garnish, then move onto the drink itself. Fill your glass with cubed ice and pour over the gin. Take the tonic out of the fridge and pour straight into the glass, filling it to around ½in/1cm. below the rim. Once the bubbles have calmed down, give everything a quick stir. Add your chosen garnish but avoid the temptation to squeeze as this can overpower the drink.

Red Snapper

GLASSWARE:

2 parts gin
4 parts tomato juice
4 dashes of Tabasco
A pinch of celery salt (optional)
½ part lemon juice
1 pinch of freshly ground black pepper
4 dashes of Worcestershire sauce
Garnish: Celery stick

Perhaps less well-known than its famous sibling, the Bloody Mary (see page 28), the Red Snapper switches up vodka for gin, adding an extra botanical element to the flavor profile which makes for a more well-rounded drink. The recipe is open to experimentation—up the amount of Tabasco if you like things spicy, while an extra dash or two of Worcestershire sauce can enhance the savory, umami content of this hair of the dog cocktail. Celery salt is also a welcome addition, but not essential if you don't have any in your spice rack.

Fill a cocktail shaker with cubed ice and add all the ingredients. Give the tin a shake and strain into a highball glass filled with cubed ice. Garnish with a large celery stick, stood upright in the glass.

Tom Collins

The Tom Collins—gin and sparkling lemonade—was probably inadvertently "invented" about five minutes after Jacob Schweppe invented soda water in 1783. Certainly, the Tom Collins was popular worldwide by the 1850s. The basic recipe is delicious, allowing the character of different gins to be compared. It is a great test-drive for a new gin—if a brand makes a good Tom Collins, then it is likely to work in a great many other cocktails.

6 parts gin
2½ parts lemon juice
3 parts simple syrup
(see page 23)
6 parts soda water
Garnish: Lemon slice,
good-quality
conserved cherry

GLASSWARE:

Lightly shake the gin, lemon juice, and syrup, together with any extra desired ingredients (see opposite) in a cocktail shaker, and strain over cubed ice into a tall highball glass. Top with soda water. Garnish with a lemon slice and a good-quality conserved cherry or other appropriate fruit.

Elderflower Collins

6 parts gin
2½ parts lemon juice
2 parts elderflower cordial
6 parts soda water
Garnish: Lemon slice,
mint sprig

GLASSWARE:

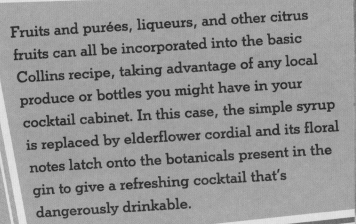

Fruits and purées, liqueurs, and other citrus fruits can all be incorporated into the basic Collins recipe, taking advantage of any local produce or bottles you might have in your cocktail cabinet. In this case, the simple syrup is replaced by elderflower cordial and its floral notes latch onto the botanicals present in the gin to give a refreshing cocktail that's dangerously drinkable.

Follow the method for the Tom Collins (opposite), but replace the simple syrup with the elderflower cordial. Top up the highball glass with soda water and garnish with a slice of lemon and a sprig of mint.

Velvet Sledgehammer

GLASSWARE:

Gin and passionfruit is a marriage made in heaven. In fact, it's so good that it's surprising no one has used it as a botanical. You can make passionfruit syrup at home but it is much easier to buy a commercial brand for consistency—Monin is a good bet. A strong, juniper-led gin works best, integrating with the fragrant passionfruit and dry apple notes from the cider.

4 parts gin
2 parts passionfruit syrup
1½ parts lemon juice
12 parts medium-dry
hard apple cider,
ideally at least 6% ABV
Garnish: Lemon slice,
apple slice or fan

Shake the gin, passionfruit syrup, and lemon juice in a cocktail shaker, then strain the mix over cubed ice into a tankard or handled beer glass. Top with the hard cider. Garnish with a lemon slice and apple slice or fan. This drink works really well as a sharing punch, just multiply the ingredients and serve in a pitcher or punch bowl.

10 mint leaves
5 parts gin
1½ parts elderflower cordial
1 part simple syrup (see page 23)
2½ parts lemon juice
Garnish: large mint sprig

English Mojito

GLASSWARE:

Although this recipe is obviously based on
a rum drink, it is arguable that the marriage
of gin and mint is even better. Elderflower is a
quintessentially English ingredient, which also
works very nicely with gin, and the cordial is
widely available and very versatile. Most gins will
work well in this recipe, but if you have either
Miller's or Hendrick's gin, please try it,
as the cucumber notes go really well together.

Gently bruise and tear the mint leaves and place in a highball glass, then
add the other ingredients and a scoop of crushed ice. Vigorously
swizzle or churn the mixture to incorporate the mint and dilute
slightly. Top up with more crushed ice to form a crown of ice proud
of the drink—this improves the presentation and also reduces
the speed of further dilution by acting as an ice duvet. Garnish
with a large mint sprig right underneath the straw.

3 cucumber slices
5 parts gin
2½ parts chamomile syrup (see box)
2 parts lemon juice
6 parts soda water
Garnish: 3 thin cucumber slices

10cc

GLASSWARE:

Originally created with Tanqueray 10, as referenced by the name, this drink pairs the warming spice of chamomile with the crisp freshness of cucumber. Tanqueray 10 uses fresh citrus peels in its recipe, alongside chamomile as a botanical, making it the perfect ingredient for this recipe. A spray of grapefruit zest will complete the picture. Although designed with a specific spirit in mind, this cocktail works well with any gin with a healthy ABV.

Muddle the cucumber in a cocktail shaker, add all the other ingredients, except for the soda water, and shake. Strain over cubed ice in a highball glass and top with the soda water. Garnish with cucumber slices.

To make the chamomile syrup, steep ¼oz (7g/4 tbsp) chamomile flowers in 1¼ cups (300ml) boiling water and let infuse for 3 minutes. Strain the contents to remove the flowers and mix the resultant liquor with 1½ cups (300g) superfine (castor) sugar and let dissolve. Cool.

Gin Sour

2 parts gin
1 part lemon juice
1 part simple syrup (see page 23)
1 egg white
Dash of Angostura bitters
Garnish: Lemon peel

This is a slightly twisted version of the traditional Gin Sour recipe, as it involves using egg white. Feel free to omit the egg if desired, but if you choose to include it you will be rewarded with an easy drinking, lightly textured drink.

GLASSWARE:  Add the ingredients except the bitters to a cocktail shaker without ice and shake hard for at least 30 seconds to allow the egg white to emulsify. Next, add cubed ice to the tin and again shake to chill the drink. Fine strain into a chilled cocktail glass and allow to settle, you should see a thick foam form at the top of the glass. To finish, add a dash of Angostura bitters.

Raspari

Created by a young bartender Vincenzo Errico to showcase one of his favorite ingredients, this cocktail is a great way to start appreciating beverage bitters like Campari. The fresh raspberries and raspberry liqueur dial back the bitterness and make a very approachable but complex drink. This drink works best with fresh raspberries in season. If unavailable, frozen raspberries or purée make a good substitute and are normally less expensive too.

3 parts gin
1 part Campari
2 parts lemon juice
5 raspberries
1 part Chambord
1 part simple syrup
(see page 23)
Garnish: Raspberry

Put all the ingredients in the cocktail shaker—there is no need to muddle the raspberries first, as they are soft enough to break up completely during shaking—with some cubed ice and shake hard. Fine strain the contents into a chilled cocktail glass to remove any seeds. Garnish with a single raspberry floating in the center of the glass.

5 raspberries
½ lime, cut into wedges,
or 1 part lime juice
3 parts gin
Dash of Chambord
Soda water, to top up
Garnish: Lime wedge
and a raspberry

In the late nineteenth century, Rickeys were all the rage, with a base liquor being softened up by a healthy does of soda water and a wedge of lime. For the Washington bartenders that created the drink—named after Colonel Joe Rickey—bourbon was the spirit of choice, before others began experimenting with gin as an alternative. Sadly, the Rickey's decline in popularity is inversely proportional to the rise of the G&T as the gin drink of the masses. However, as is the case with many long-forgotten cocktails, drink historians have revived the venerable Rickey and tinkered with it to invent interesting alternatives like this version.

Raspberry Rickey

GLASSWARE:

There are two ways to make this drink: a rustic-looking version or something a bit more presentable. If you're the rough and ready type, place the raspberries and the lime wedges in a highball glass and muddle to release the juices. Add the gin and Chambord and mix together before adding a few ice cubes and topping up with soda water.

For a more refined version, place the raspberries in a cocktail shaker and add the lime juice, gin, and Chambord. Muddle the ingredients together and fine strain the liquid into a highball glass. Fill the glass with cracked ice and top up with the soda water. To finish, garnish with a wedge of lime and a raspberry.

Aviation

3 parts gin
1 part lemon juice
1 part maraschino liqueur
Dash of crème de violette
Garnish: lemon twist

Harking back to the age of those magnificent men and their flying machines, the Aviation first appeared at the start of the twentieth century and is credited to Hugo Ensslin, the head bartender at New York's celebrated Hotel Wallick, who featured the drink in his 1916 book Recipes for Mixed Drinks. The cocktail disappeared for a while due to the fact that crème de violette, which gives the drink its distinct blue tint, was not readily available. Thankfully that's changed over recent years and Aviations have become increasingly common on menus at many quality drinking establishments.

Put all the ingredients into a cocktail shaker along with some cubed ice. Give the ingredients a hard shake for around 15–20 seconds, until the contents are chilled and the ice diluted to take the edge off the alcohol. Fine strain carefully into a chilled cocktail glass to remove any particles of ice and lemon, then garnish with a piece of lemon twist.

Casino

As mentioned opposite for the Aviation, crème de violette isn't the easiest ingredient to get hold of and it still takes a bit of searching to uncover a bottle. If you can't track down the violet liqueur, you can still make the drink without it and the resulting Casino cocktail is the perfect mix of sweet and citrus. The maraschino provides a pleasing sugary hit that is counterbalanced by the citrus zing of the lemon juice and orange bitters.

3 parts gin
1 part lemon juice
1 part maraschino liqueur
2 dashes of orange bitters
Garnish: Orange peel or good quality cocktail cherry

Take your cocktail shaker, add the ingredients, and fill with cubed ice. Give the tin a good shake to cool everything down before straining into a chilled cocktail glass. Take your orange peel and give it a twist or alternatively spear your cocktail cherry onto a cocktail stick/toothpick and add to the glass.

GLASSWARE:

Corpse Reviver No. 2

1 part gin
1 part orange liqueur
1 part lemon juice
1 part dry vermouth
Dash of absinthe
Garnish: Lemon peel

GLASSWARE:

Here's an adaptation of another Harry Craddock classic, which is designed to shake off the shackles of a particularly menacing hangover and have you back on your feet after just a few sips. The original recipe calls for Kina Lillet, which is no longer available, but any brand of dry vermouth will be a perfectly serviceable replacement.

Before you start, decide how you want to include the absinthe. You can either add it to the mix with the other ingredients, or swirl the spirit in the cocktail glass and discard before you start on the rest of the drink. Once you've made your decision, add all the ingredients into a cocktail shaker filled with cubed ice and shake hard for around 20 seconds. Strain the liquid into the chilled (possibly absinthe-rinsed) cocktail glass and garnish with the lemon peel, squeezing it first to release some of the citrus oils.

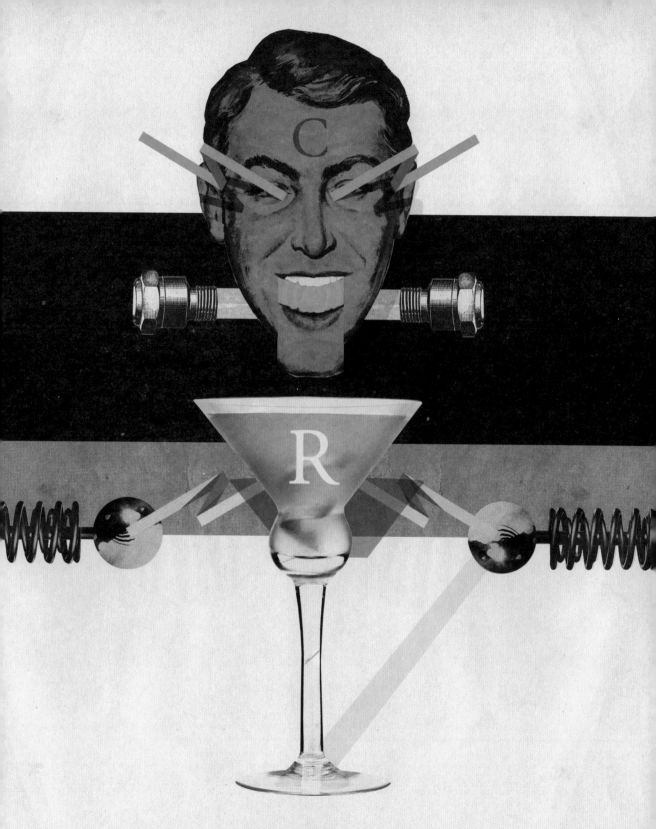

Lime wedge
Salt
2 parts tequila
1 part orange liqueur
½ part fresh lime juice
Garnish: Lime wedge
or wheel

Margarita

GLASSWARE:

The Margarita is the world's most popular cocktail—sipped leisurely by discerning drinkers at achingly cool urban cocktail lounges and downed with abandon by party animals looking to take advantage of happy hour. Given the Margarita's ubiquity, it goes without saying that there's a right and a wrong way to make one. The first sin is using cheap tequila, the sort of paint stripper that's responsible for some of the most excruciatingly painful hangovers imaginable. Always use 100% agave tequila, it's actually pleasant to drink. Secondly, never buy pre-made Margarita mix—the difference that fresh lime juice makes can not be overstated. No one with even the slightest interest in making tasty cocktails should use anything other than fresh.

Start by preparing your glass. Rub a wedge of lime around the rim of a chilled cocktail glass and roll the edge of the glass in salt. Add the tequila, orange liqueur, and fresh lime juice to a cocktail shaker filled with cubed ice. Shake sharply and strain into the glass. Garnish with a wedge or wheel of lime.

SALTING A RIM

A well-salted rim should only have salt on the outside of the glass, otherwise the contents can become unpalatably saline. To do this, start by rubbing a lime wedge around the rim to moisten the glass and provide some liquid for the salt to stick to. Next, pour a couple of tablespoons of salt (kosher salt is best) into a small plate. Take the cocktail glass and roll the rim in the salt until the whole edge is covered. With a paper towel remove any salt that's managed to find its way to the inside of the rim and you're ready to go.

Lagerita

Given the explosion of the craft brewing movement in recent years, it's unsurprising that bartenders are experimenting more with beer as a cocktail ingredient. This twist on the Margarita uses a classic Mexican beer like Corona or Modelo alongside the traditional ingredients of tequila and orange liqueur to make a refreshing long drink.

2 parts tequila
1 part orange liqueur
4 parts Mexican lager
1 part fresh lime juice
Garnish: Lime wedge

Add all the ingredients apart from the lager to a cocktail shaker and shake with cubed ice. Pour into a highball glass filled with ice and top up with the lager. Garnish with a lime wedge.

5 parts tequila

1 part fresh lime juice

1 part fresh pink grapefruit juice

Grapefruit soda, to top up (Ting or Squirt are great brands)

Garnish: Lime and/or grapefruit twist

Grapefruit and tequila is one of the greatest ingredient combinations known to man, as the Paloma expertly demonstrates. This version tweaks the Mexican original by adding fresh grapefruit juice alongside the grapefruit-flavored soda, adding a pleasing acidity to the mix.

Paloma

GLASSWARE:

Start by salting the rim of a highball glass. Next, fill the glass with ice cubes and pour in the tequila, lime juice, and grapefruit juice. To finish, top up with the grapefruit soda and garnish with a lime and/or grapefruit twist.

Grapefruit Cobbler

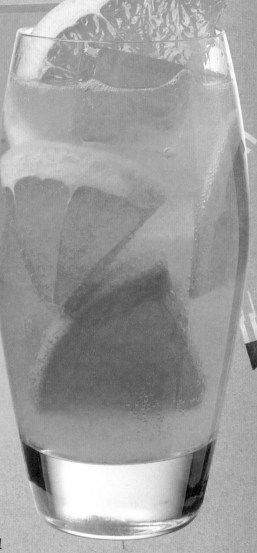

This drink works best if you squeeze the grapefruit juice just before you make it, as the pasteurization process used in cartoned juices ruins the delicate flavors of the grapefruit. Luckily ripe grapefruits yield a lot of juice, so squeezing is not too onerous. This drink also works very well in a punch bowl; keep it cool with a large lump of ice, perhaps with slices of grapefruit frozen inside.

3 slices pink grapefruit

5 parts tequila

1 part lemon juice

2 parts simple syrup (see page 23)

7 parts pink grapefruit juice

Garnish: Grapefruit slice, cut into quarters

Muddle the grapefruit slices in a large highball glass, then add the remaining ingredients and some crushed ice. Swizzle and garnish with another slice of pink grapefruit.

5 parts tequila
3 parts simple syrup (see page 23)
2½ parts fresh lime juice
6 parts soda water
Garnish: Lime wedge

GLASSWARE:

Pepito Collins

The Collins is one of the most versatile cocktails around, with versions in existence for almost all spirits. Here's the recipe for the tequila Collins, which has been dubbed Pedro to honor the spirit's Hispanic roots.

Pour the tequila, simple syrup, and lime juice into a highball glass filled with ice cubes. Top up with the soda water and add a lime wedge to garnish.

Dragon

10 white grapes
1 part fresh lime juice
1½ parts elderflower cordial
5 parts tequila
Garnish: Half a grape

Here's a drink to convert tequila sceptics. The spirit's vegetal qualities provide a solid backbone to support the floral notes of the elderflower cordial, which in turn works beautifully with the sweet white grapes and the fresh tang of the lime. The Dragon has better balance than an Olympic gymnast and is an ideal summer sipper.

Muddle the grapes in a cocktail shaker then add the lime juice, elderflower cordial, and tequila. Add some cubed ice and shake hard for 15 seconds. Fine strain into a cocktail glass and add the grape garnish to the rim.

GLASSWARE:

El Diablo

2 parts tequila
1 part blackcurrant liqueur
1 part fresh lime juice
Ginger beer, to top up
Garnish: Lime wheel

Spicy, fiery, fruity... what's not to like about this classic which dates back to the 1940s.

GLASSWARE:

This drink can be assembled directly in the glass—add the blackcurrant liqueur at the end and watch it bleed through the ice cubes creating an attractive appearance. For a more evenly mixed drink add the tequila, liqueur, and lime to a cocktail shaker and fill with ice cubes. Give the contents a solid shake and strain into a highball glass filled with ice. Carefully pour in the ginger beer to fill the glass and garnish with a lime wheel.

Bloody Maria

GLASSWARE:

2 parts tequila
4 parts tomato juice
4 dashes of Tabasco
A pinch of celery salt (optional)
½ part fresh lemon juice
1 pinch of freshly ground black pepper
4 dashes of Worcestershire sauce
Garnish: Lemon wheel

Just as tequila can be held responsible for your hangover, so too can the spirit be used to cure that pounding headache. The Bloody Maria is a pick-me-up that, for many, trumps the original vodka Bloody Mary. The added spiciness and fruitiness found in blanco tequilas mirror those flavors found in the other ingredients.

Add all the ingredients to a cocktail shaker and fill with ice cubes. Give the contents a quick shake and strain into a highball glass filled with ice. Garnish with a lemon wheel.

2½ parts tequila
1 part white crème de cacao
1 part light/single cream
¼ part grenadine
Garnish: Fresh raspberries
(optional)

Silk Stocking

GLASSWARE:

This tequila drink was invented during the 1920s in the USA, at a time when cocktails were often given names revelling in innuendo and sensuality. It's an after-dinner drink, which is a name often given to cocktails that use cream as an ingredient.

Pour the ingredients into a cocktail shaker and fill with cubed ice. Give the ingredients a good shake to chill, and then strain into a rocks glass filled with ice cubes. Whether you garnish or not is entirely up to you, but a raspberry or two on a cocktail stick/toothpick can look the part.

Here's a drink that cocktail aficionados wouldn't be seen dead imbibing. It's about as cool as a sauna in the Sahara desert but in some weird hipster twist does that make it ironically cool again? Possibly not, but you should probably try a Tequila Sunrise once in your life just to say you have.

1 part tequila
3 parts orange juice
½ part grenadine
Garnish: orange slice and a cocktail cherry—the lurid red kind

Tequila Sunrise

GLASSWARE:

Fill a highball glass with ice cubes and pour in the tequila and the orange juice. Next, slowly pour in the grenadine, which should sink to the bottom of the glass, giving the sunrise effect. For such a kitsch drink it would be rude not to go big on garnishes. Usually you would be well-advised to steer clear of bright red cocktail "cherries," but in this case it just seems right. Add an orange wedge and you are good to go.

Toreador

GLASSWARE:

2 parts tequila
1 part fresh lime juice
1 part apricot liqueur
Garnish: Lime wedge

A Toreador is a bullfighter and much like its namesake this cocktail is bold, sharp, and blessed with excellent balance. It is a cousin of the Margarita (see page 108), but switches out the orange liqueur for apricot liqueur. This substitution is a smart move as the characteristics of the stone fruit bring a pleasing complexity to the finished article.

Fill a cocktail shaker with a couple of handfuls of cubed ice and pour in the tequila, lime juice, and apricot liqueur. Give everything a good shake and strain into a chilled cocktail glass. To finish, add the lime wedge to the rim of the glass as a garnish.

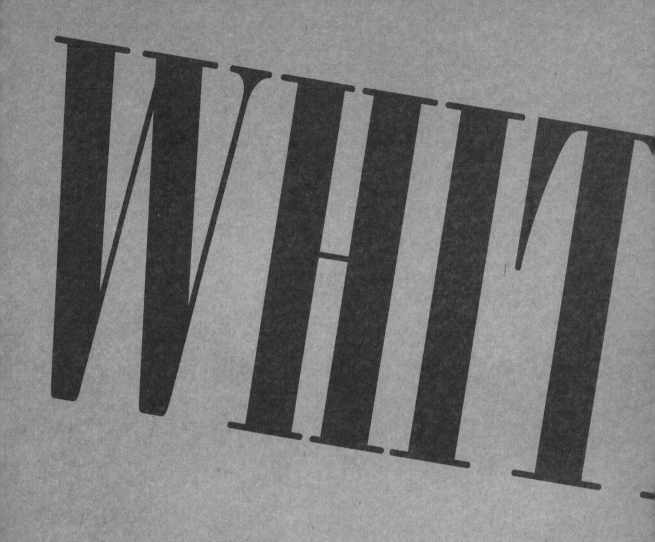

Daiquiri

A well-made Daiquiri is as delicious a cocktail as you can experience, but is there such a thing as the perfect Daiquiri recipe? It's a question that has bugged all the best bartenders and serious debates have occurred across bars around the world on what constitutes the ultimate formula for combining rum, lime, and sugar. The version below is merely a starting point for your own quest to find the holy grail that is the perfect Daiquiri—have fun on your journey.

5 parts white rum
2 parts lime juice
1½ parts simple syrup
(see page 23)
Garnish: Lime twist
or wedge

Add the rum, lime juice, and simple syrup to a cocktail shaker and fill with cubed ice. Give all the ingredients a good shake to cool before fine straining into a chilled cocktail glass. Add a lime twist or wedge to the rim of the cocktail glass as a garnish and enjoy.

4 parts white rum
½ part maraschino liqueur
1 part grapefruit juice
1½ parts simple syrup
(see page 23)
1 part fresh lime juice
Garnish: Lime peel

It's fitting that such a legendary literary figure should have his name inextricably linked to such a legendary cocktail as the Daiquiri. For Hemingway's version, also known as the Papa Doble, the barman at Havana's famous Floridita bar created a Daiquiri that used double the rum and maraschino liqueur as a sweetener, taking into account the writer's dislike of sugar. This version is widely regarded to be a bit too punchy, so modern versions reinstate the sugar to address balance issues similar to those Hemingway faced after one too many of his eponymous cocktail.

Hemingway Daiquiri

Take a cocktail shaker and add in all the ingredients along with a generous handful of cubed ice. Put the lid on and give everything a sharp shake for 10–15 seconds until everything is combined. Fine strain the contents into a chilled cocktail glass and garnish with a lime peel.

GLASSWARE:

Strawberry Daiquiri

Here's a Daiquiri for people who claim not to like Daiquiris. The addition of strawberries gives an extra element of sugar that softens the sharpness of the lime in the traditional version, making the drink a little more palatable to those who prefer their cocktails a little sweeter.

GLASSWARE:

4 strawberries
2½ parts white rum
1 parts lime juice
1 parts simple syrup
(see page 23)
Garnish: strawberry

Place the two strawberries in a cocktail shaker and muddle to release the juices. Once that's done, add the rum, lime juice, and simple syrup along with a handful of ice cubes. Give the ingredients a shake for around 15 seconds and fine strain the liquid into a chilled cocktail glass to remove any strawberry seeds. Garnish with a strawberry on the rim of the glass.

4 parts rum
1 part orange liqueur
2 parts Demerara syrup
3 parts heavy (double) cream
2 dashes of Angostura bitters
1 pinch of ground cinnamon
1 small egg yolk
Garnish: Cinnamon stick,
freshly grated nutmeg

Caribbean Flip

GLASSWARE:

This warming, spiced after-dinner drink is rich and luxurious and not a little boozy. Any rum can be used with the result of very different flavor profiles—dark rums produce deep, rich notes of spice and brown sugar while lighter rums bring out orange notes and the aromatics from the bitters. If you are feeling very brave, a little dash of stout in the recipe is a wonderful thing.

Shake all the ingredients very hard in a cocktail shaker with cubed ice for at least 30 seconds; the harder you shake, the lighter the texture will be. Strain into a chilled wine glass and garnish with a long stick of cinnamon and some freshly grated nutmeg.

Mojito

GLASSWARE:

8 mint leaves
2 parts simple syrup
(see page 23)
5 parts white rum
2 parts lime juice
Garnish: Mint sprig

With origins dating back to the 16th century, the Mojito—or El Draque as it was called back then—is one of the world's most famous and celebrated drinks. And it's hard to argue with its position at the top table of the cocktail world—light, refreshing, and far too easy to drink, this is a guaranteed crowd-pleaser.

Take the mint leaves and add them to a highball glass along with the simple syrup. Muddle the two ingredients together to release the oils in the leaves—be gentle and don't bash the leaves too hard as this will bruise them. Next, add the remaining ingredients, top up the glass with crushed ice, and give everything a quick stir to combine. To finish, take a spring of mint, slap it against the palm of your hand to release the mint oils for aroma, and add it to the glass as a garnish.

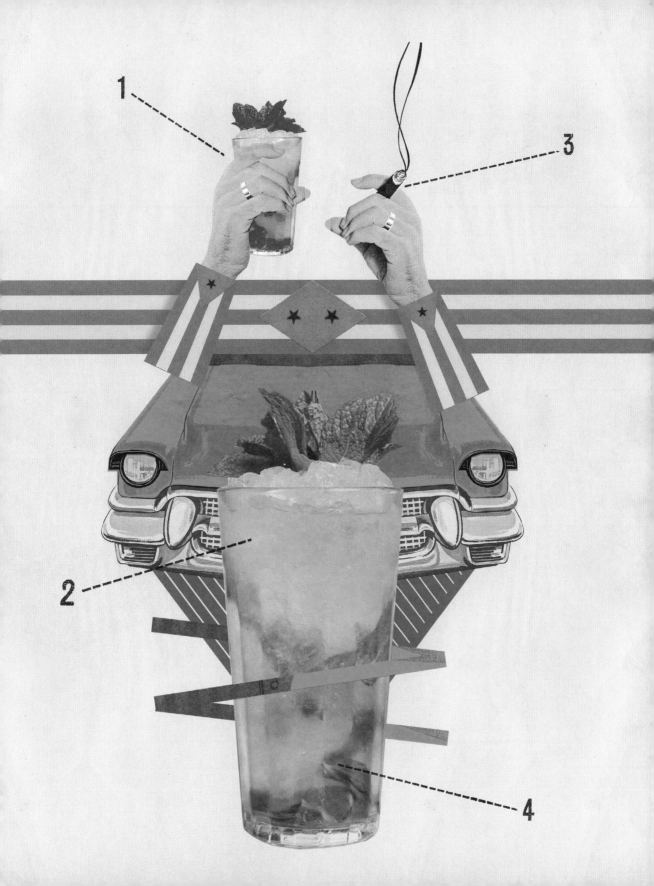

Pedro Collins

GLASSWARE:

2 parts rum
1 part lime juice
½ part simple syrup
Soda water, to top up
2-3 dashes of Angostura bitters (optional)
Garnish: Lime wheel

You've already met Tom (see page 94) and his Mexican cousin Pepito (see page 113), now it's time to spend a leisurely evening in the company of Pedro, head of the Cuban branch of the Collins clan.

Fill a highball glass with some cubed ice and pour in the rum, lime juice, and simple syrup. Top up the glass with soda water and the Angostura bitters (if using). Add a straw for further mixing (and drinking!) if desired, then garnish with a lime wheel.

Cuba Libre

½ a lime, cut into wedges
1 part white rum
3 parts cola
Garnish: Spent lime wedges

Rum, coke, and lime; that's it. This has to be one of the quickest and easiest drinks in the cocktail canon, but that's not to say it's not worth the effort (or lack thereof) to make one, because there's a certain appeal to its sweet simplicity.

GLASSWARE:

Fill the highball with ice and squeeze the lime wedges over the glass to release the juice. Drop the drained wedges into the glass for a rustic garnish, then pour in the rum and top up with cola. Stir gently and serve.

2 parts white rum
2 parts pineapple juice
2 dashes of grenadine
1 dash of maraschino liqueur
Garnish: Lime twist

GLASSWARE:

Considered the Angelina Jolie of her day, Mary Pickford was an Oscar-winning movie star who was considered "America's sweetheart" during the Prohibition era. So it's appropriate that following a visit to Havana she has a cocktail named after her that's sweet on the palate.

Mary Pickford

Pour the ingredients into a cocktail shaker and fill with cubed ice. Give everything a decent shake to combine and fine strain into a chilled cocktail glass. To finish, garnish with a twist of lime on the side of the glass.

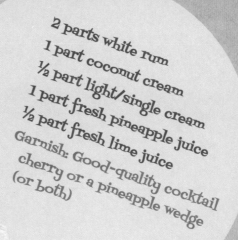

2 parts white rum
1 part coconut cream
½ part light/single cream
1 part fresh pineapple juice
½ part fresh lime juice
Garnish: Good-quality cocktail cherry or a pineapple wedge (or both)

Piña Colada

GLASSWARE:

Much like watching reality TV shows, listening to show tunes, or enjoying clandestine visits to McDonalds, the Piña Colada is a bit of a guilty pleasure. These days umbrellas in your drinks and enormous pineapple garnishes are frowned upon by the cocktail cognoscenti, but sometimes those buttoned-up stiffs take things a bit too seriously. And who cares what they think when you're sipping one of these at a beachside bar in some tropical paradise.

Add all the ingredients to a blender with a scoop of crushed ice and blitz until combined. Pour into a highball glass and garnish with a thick chunk of pineapple and/or cocktail cherry.

2 parts white rum
Pulp of 1 passionfruit
1 part fresh orange juice
4 parts lemonade

Passionfruit Rum Punch

GLASSWARE:

Passionfruit is widely grown in the same Caribbean countries that produce rum so it makes perfect sense to use the sweet fruit as a key ingredient in a punch. You could use golden rum but I prefer the slightly more delicate taste of white rum. The recipe can be easily scaled up for a punch.

Half fill a highball glass with ice and add in the rum, passionfruit pulp, and orange juice. Top up with lemonade and give everything a stir to combine the flavors. Serve immediately.

Ti' Punch

Juice of ½ lime
½ part cane sugar syrup
3 parts rhum agricole

This petit, or little punch gets its name from the French Antilles islands of Guadeloupe and Martinique, where the cocktail is widely enjoyed as an aperitif. To make a genuine version you need to use white rhum agricole, a style unique to the region that is distilled using sugar cane rather than the more traditional molasses. The below quantities are a guide, so try experimenting with different ratios to find your perfect blend.

Take a rocks glass, squeeze in the juice of half a lime, and drop in the shell. Next, add the cane sugar syrup and the rum and give the ingredients a good stir to mix everything together. Traditionally, locals drink their Ti Punches straight up with no ice, so give that a go if you want to be authentic. Alternatively, a few ice cubes chill everything down and add a little dilution, making for a less intense and more refreshing punch.

Jamaican Breeze

GLASSWARE:

Fruity, fiery, and aromatic, the Jamaican Breeze is testament to Jamaican rum's ability to hold its own when mixed with different flavors.

2 fresh ginger slices
2 parts white rum
3 parts cranberry juice
3 parts pineapple juice
Dash of Angostura bitters
Garnish: Lime wheel

Pound the fresh ginger and rum together in the bottom of a cocktail shaker with a barspoon or muddler, then add ice and the remaining ingredients. Shake and strain into a rocks glass filled with ice. Garnish with a lime wheel.

2 parts white rum
1 part lime juice
½ part orange liqueur
2 dashes of maraschino liqueur
Garnish: Lime zest

During the mid-20th century, Tiki culture—that is the celebration of the South Pacific—was all the rage in the United States, spawning a trend for exotic cocktails. One of the key names in Tiki culture was Trader Vic's, a chain of restaurants that produced Bar-Tender's Guide featuring the Beachcomber—a take on the Daiquiri with the addition of a little orange and maraschino liqueurs.

Beachcomber

GLASSWARE:

Add the ingredients to a cocktail shaker filled with ice cubes and give everything a shake for around 10–15 seconds. Once the contents are cooled, fine strain into a chilled cocktail glass and garnish with some lime zest.

1 lime, cut into wedges
2 brown sugar cubes
2 parts cachaça
Simple syrup (see page 23),
to taste

Caipirinha

GLASSWARE:

More Brazilian than Neymar samba dancing on Ipanema Beach in a pair of Havaianas flip flops, the Caipirinha is the national cocktail of Brazil and is consumed in bars from Recife to Rio de Janiero. The key ingredient is cachaça, a spirit indigenous to Brazil that is distilled directly from the juice of sugar cane— similar to the rhum agricole made in the French Antilles. When combined with the sweet sugar and the sour limes it makes for a beguiling cocktail.

Drop the lime wedges and sugar cubes into a rocks glass, squeezing the limes as you go, then pound well with a pestle. Fill the glass with crushed ice and add the cachaça. Stir vigorously and add sugar syrup, to taste.

Raspberry Batida

Batidas are a hit with drinkers in Brazil but so far their blend of fresh fruit, condensed milk, and cachaça remains relatively unknown to the rest of the world. The options on offer are numerous, with coconut, passion fruit, and even the local Brazilian acai berries being an option. For this version, the readily available raspberry does the job nicely.

GLASSWARE:

8 raspberries
2 parts cachaça
1 part condensed milk
½ part simple syrup (see page 23)
Garnish: 1 raspberry

Put the raspberries in a cocktail shaker and muddle to release the juices. Add the cachaça, condensed milk, sugar syrup, and some cubed ice then shake hard. Strain into a highball filled with crushed ice, stir, and garnish with a raspberry on the rim of the glass.

½ apple

2 parts cachaça

½ part cinnamon liqueur

Dash of fresh lime or lemon juice

Dash of simple syrup (see page 23)

Garnish: Apple slice or apple-peel twist (optional)

Here's a Brazilian take on a classic, using cachaça instead of the more traditional gin or vodka. The spirit on its own can be a little rough around the edges, so fresh apple is deployed to tame the fiery Brazilian beast and the cinnamon liqueur plays an excellent supporting role.

Azure Martini

GLASSWARE:

Remove any tough core from the apple half with a knife, place into a cocktail shaker, and pound to release the flavor. Add crushed ice and the remaining ingredients, shake and strain through a sieve into a frosted cocktail glass. Garnish with an apple slice or apple-peel twist if you're feeling fancy.

1 apricot, cut into wedges

1 lime, cut into wedges

1 part sugar syrup
(see page 23)

3 parts cachaça

Garnish: Lime wedge

Given the growth in popularity of the Caipirinha and the fact that it's become far easier to get hold of a bottle of cachaça, there has been an ever-increasing number of fruit variations of the original appearing on cocktail menus. This version uses apricots, which have a floral and sweet flavor that stands up solidly to the lime.

Apricot Caipirinha

Muddle the apricot and lime wedges in a cocktail shaker. Add the sugar syrup and cachaça and a handful of cracked ice cubes then shake hard. Pour everything into a rocks glass but don't strain—you want a rustic-looking drink— and garnish with a lime wedge.

GLASSWARE:

Brazilian Drum

GLASSWARE:

½ lime, cut into wedges
2 teaspoons cinnamon sugar
2 parts cachaça

This take on a Caipirinha uses cinnamon sugar to enhance the end result. To make cinnamon sugar, simply mix ¼ cup (50g) sugar with 1 tablespoon ground cinnamon.

Muddle the lime and cinnamon sugar in a rock glass. Add crushed ice and cachaça and stir.

Index